Untold Stories

Untold Stories

How I Survived a Child Porn Ring

Timmy Fielding

iUniverse, Inc.
Bloomington

Untold Stories
How I Survived a Child Porn Ring

iUniverse books may be ordered through booksellers or by contacting:

iUniverse
1663 Liberty Drive
Bloomington, IN 47403
www.iuniverse.com
1-800-Authors (1-800-288-4677)

Because of the dynamic nature of the Internet, any web addresses or links contained in this book may have changed since publication and may no longer be valid. The views expressed in this work are solely those of the author and do not necessarily reflect the views of the publisher, and the publisher hereby disclaims any responsibility for them.

Any people depicted in stock imagery provided by Thinkstock are models, and such images are being used for illustrative purposes only.
Certain stock imagery © Thinkstock.

ISBN: 978-1-4620-4714-7 (sc)
ISBN: 978-1-4620-4715-4 (hc)
ISBN: 978-1-4620-4716-1 (ebk)

Library of Congress Control Number: 2011914238

Printed in the United States of America

iUniverse rev. date: 10/12/2011

As I left Brian's house, I was devastated. I wondered who would ever love me like he did. I was thinking of all the good times, dismissing all the bad times in my mind. For me, the good outweighed the bad. My heart was breaking, and the tears began to flow; I couldn't have stopped them anyways. How would I ever make it without him? When things got bad at home where would I turn to? Where would I escape? I didn't want to leave this little bit of safety that I had become used to. It wasn't my idea to move. Heck, I didn't even have a say in this decision that had changed my life so much. Sometimes it really sucked to be a kid. I was carrying on and talking to myself and realized that I was almost to my old house.

I dried my face off with my shirt and tried to put on a happy face for my family.

"Where have you been?" my father demanded.

"Saying good-bye," I exclaimed.

His voice softened just a little and he said, "Get in the truck."

My brother, Tom, made me sit in the middle next to Dad.

I asked, "Dad, how far is it to our new house from here?"

"Let's see. We'll check the mileage and the time. There's 59,216 miles on the truck now and it is 10:45. Let's see how long it takes us."

I watched the roads carefully, trying to remember names and landmarks I could recognize later. I couldn't leave breadcrumbs like Hansel and Gretel. So I paid close attention, just in case I ever needed to come back. I thought of Brian all the way to the new house.

We pulled into the driveway and Dad said, "Well its 11:09, Timmy, so how long did it take to get here?"

"Twenty four minutes."

"Very good, and the odometer reads 59,230 miles. How many miles is that?"

"Fourteen miles," Tom blurted out.

"Very good," Dad said.

I thought to myself, *that's not too far*. I was really nervous about the move, and the more I looked around at the new house and the new neighborhood, the more I realized the huge difference between it and our old neighborhood. We really had lived in a poor neighborhood, almost poor enough to call it a ghetto. I had never thought of it that way before, and I had never looked at us as being poor. My dad always worked hard, and we always had food and some clothes. I could tell that moving to Yorba Linda was a huge step up for us.

I loved our new house; it was twice as big as the old one. Mom and Dad bought a lot of new furniture, and it made the house look really nice. When you walked, into the foyer, and Dad put a new grandfather clock there; he was proud of it. To the right was a big living room. Mom put up new curtains, and the couch and love seat had big, oversized, fluffy pillows on it. Dad had a large recliner that nobody else was allowed to sit in. We now had a large, wooden coffee table and new light stands. In the dining room, we had a new table and a beautiful cherry wood hutch that Mom put new china inside it. My brother and I got new bedroom sets, and that had never happened before. My room was the first bedroom you passed when you came in the house and Tommy's was the next. Mom and Dad's bedroom was in the back of the house, and this gave them privacy.

Mom and Dad seemed happy, and that night, Mom cooked the family a really nice dinner. Everyone sat around the table eating and laughing and really enjoying the atmosphere of the new home. Mom was in a great mood. I began to think that maybe things could be different, maybe this is what we needed. Just maybe, we could be a normal family now.

That night, I took a hot bath before bedtime, and it was quiet and relaxing. I lay there enjoying the warmth of the water. I laid my head back and fell asleep.

Suddenly, I heard a loud bang on the door, and it jarred me awake. "Get out! It's my turn! You've been in there long enough!" Tom yelled.

I noticed the water was cold as I jumped out of the tub and put a towel around me. I was shivering and trying to dry off quickly.

"Open this door right now!" Mom yelled this time.

I unlocked the door, and Mom pushed it open so hard that it hit the wall. Before I knew what was happening she reached out and slapped me as hard as she could across the face. Then she grabbed my hair and dragged me down the hall to my room. All the while, she yelled and screamed how bad I was. With her free hand, she was swinging the belt with all her strength. The towel fell off as she threw me into my room head first. I hit the floor and rolled away from her. She got into position to start the beating.

I rolled in a ball to hide and protect myself; I was embarrassed at being naked. But that was the least of my worries, as the pain started and increased with each hit. She was using all her might and hit high and low trying not to miss any spots. I was begging and screaming for her to stop, and this just made her madder. I lay there crying and moaning. Finally, she stopped and turned and walked out the bedroom door. I lay there for a few minutes then crawled to my bed and got under the sheets. At that moment, I knew the move to Yorba Linda—the better house, the new furniture—none of it had changed her. She was the same person she had always been; the same anger and the same rage had just moved to a new location.

Monday came quickly and it was our first day at the new school. We lived in a housing track in the hills. We were almost at the top, and the school was at the bottom. It was a long walk and lots of different streets to learn. It was easy going downhill to school but a lot harder going back up at the end of the day. Since it was the first day, Mom took us to school and did her usual bullshit good mother routine. Tom would be going to junior high, and I was going into the fourth grade. Tom's school was in a different direction than mine.

We went to my school first and checked in at the office. After we got signed in, the principal came out to meet us. "Hi, I'm Mr. Davies, the principal," he said.

Mr. Davies was a large man in every way. He was tall and fat and was completely bald, but he had a kind face and smiling eyes. He looked at me and asked, "What's your name?"

I replied, "Timmy."

He stuck out his hand and shook my hand firmly; it almost hurt.

"I'm Mrs. Fielding's." My mom introduced herself, and they shook hands.

"Mrs. Fielding's, we haven't received any of Timmy's transcripts yet from his last school. What grade are you in, Timmy?"

"Fourth grade' sir"

"Well then, I know just where to put you. Ms. Right's class has an opening. You will like her a lot. She is a very good teacher, and she is really nice."

I smiled

Mr. Davies teased, "Now, Timmy, you're not a troublemaker, are you?"

I quickly answered, "No, sir. I am not."

Mom got mad because the principal seemed to like me. "Well I have to go."

Mr. Davies replied, "It was nice to meet you."

"Yes, you too" She looks at me making a point. "Timmy, you behave." Then she turned on her heels and walked away.

This was the first time she hadn't stayed to meet the teacher, and I was glad she left so quickly. It gave her less of a chance to humiliate me.

"Well Timmy, let's go meet your new teacher, Ms. Right," Mr. Davies said as we walked down the hallway.

I felt like the lamb being led to the slaughter.

Mr. Davies opened the door, and we walked through. The whole class fell completely silent, and everyone was staring at me.

"Ms. Right, this is Timmy Fielding's. He just moved from Norwalk," Mr. Davies said, introducing me.

Ms. Right replied, "Well, Timmy, it is very nice to meet you."

We shook hands. Then she turned toward the class and told them, "Class, this is Timmy. Let's make him feel at home." She pointed to a desk in the back of the room that I could sit in. I smiled and walked to my seat and sat down.

The boy ahead of me turned around and introduced himself. "My name is Denny. Nice to meet you"

Everyone in the class all had his or her head turned to the back to get a better look at the new kid.

Ms. Right called the class to order. She could tell I was uncomfortable with all the attention. "Now take out your reading book," the teacher said. She walked back to my desk and handed me the book I needed and winked at me. I smiled back at her.

Ms. Right was pretty, and all the boys were nuts about her. She was tall with long brown hair and the prettiest brown eyes with golden flecks in them. She was slender and in her early thirties.

When the lunch bell rang, we lined up and after we quieted down, we walked to the lunch room. All the kids seemed really nice to me. I got a lunch tray and walked to the first open table. Denny called out to me, "No, Timmy, come eat with us." This made me feel good, and I moved to his table. I made quite a few friends that day, and after school, Denny asked me if I wanted to go to his house and play. I knew I wasn't going home, so I quickly agreed.

He didn't live far from the school; his housing track was across from the school. We walked down the street and crossed a busy street using the light. On the other side of the street were a Vons supermarket and a Thrifty's drugstore. Denny was about my height and slender like me. He had black hair with a flattop haircut and blue eyes. He had a baby face that the girls at school thought he was really cute. Denny lived in a very large house that was less than a year old. It looked like a two-story model house, and the yard was done to perfection. I was afraid to walk in. I thought my very presence would dirty it.

Denny said, "Come on in."

I reached down and started taking my shoes off, and he said, "You don't have to do that."

I shook my head and looked around and said, "Oh yes, I do."

The foyer was marble and the carpet was white. It reminded me of Rick and Todd's house.

Denny yelled to his mom that he was home. She called him into the kitchen where she was baking. We walked down a hall to the kitchen, and as we entered, Denny introduced me. "Mom, this is Timmy."

She looked up surprised, not expecting anyone extra and looked me over. She liked what she saw because she smiled nicely at me. She introduces herself to me. "Hi, I'm Mrs. Ross. Nice to meet you"

I walked over to her and shook her hand.

"Well, Timmy, you are very polite," she said. "Oh, look, you even took off your shoes; how considerate of you."

"Thank you, Mrs. Ross."

She smiled at me and said, "I hope you teach Denny some of these manners." I smiled back at her and she continued on, "Why don't you guys go play, and I will call you when the cookies are done."

I followed Denny to his room. When I walked in, I couldn't believe what I saw. "Holy shit" I exclaimed. This is your room?"

"Yeah, do you like it?"

I walked around the room answering, "Do I like it? Who wouldn't? It's great!"

A train set was built on the shelves on the walls so you could flip it and switch the train tracks as it went around the room. There were tunnels it would go through, smoke that came out of the locomotive stacks, and every once in a while, the whistle would blow. His bunk bed was a fire truck; the cab of the truck completely covered the top of the bed and windows looked out into the room. A desk was built in the back of the fire truck. You entered through the back door, you could turn on a light switch inside. It was the coolest thing I had ever seen. He had his own TV and stereo and a couple of beanbags to sit on. "Denny, this is the coolest room I've ever seen!" I told him again.

We ended up playing with Lego's and built a tower as high as we could.

Time went by quick, and Denny's mom brought the cookies and some milk to his room so we could eat in there.

"So Timmy where do you live" Mrs. Ross asked me. I explained as best I could, and she said, "Well that is kind of far. You'll need a ride home."

"No. It's not as far as it sounds."

"Well you better call your mom and tell her where you are."

"We just moved here, and the phone isn't hooked up yet."

"You'd better leave because your mom is probably worried about you by now."

I agreed with her and thanked her for the milk and cookies. I also thanked Denny for letting me come over. The last thing she said was, "You really are a polite kid." I smiled and said good-bye and left.

I walked out of the house and down the street to the crosswalk. I was thinking about what a great day it had been—a lot better than I'd thought it was going to be. I wanted to share it with someone. I looked across the street and saw a pay phone in front of Thrifty. I knew what I wanted to do; I wanted to call Brian. What could it hurt? Wouldn't he be happy for me? I knew he'd said we couldn't see each other, but what would a phone call matter? I reasoned with myself all the way to the pay phone.

I put in a dime and dialed his number, and the operator asked for an additional quarter so I put that in too.

The phone rang, and Brian answered saying, "Hello."

I said, "Brian, it's me, Timmy."

There was a long silence on the phone, and when he finally answered, his voice was distant and cold. "Timmy, how did you call me?"

Confused by the question I answered, "I'm at a pay phone, and I know how to use a phone, Brian."

He asked oddly, "Why are you calling me?"

Trying to gain back lost ground, I answered cheerfully, "I had a great day and wanted to tell you about it."

He wasn't swayed by my cheerfulness, "I don't care, Timmy. We had an agreement that you would not call me or come over again. It's too dangerous for you." Then he just hung up on me.

I couldn't believe it. I was shocked, and my heart hurt. I didn't understand. I thought he would be glad that all the hard work he had done to make me popular had paid off. Now I knew how to make friends and get along better with other people. I wasn't as shy, and he was the one who had helped build my confidence. If he loved me like a son like he said, how could he just hang up on me like that? It seemed I would never understand the people in my life that I loved.

The walk home was uphill all the way, and even though I was in good shape, it was still harder than I thought it would be. But I knew it would make me stronger and I would get used to it. The only problem was that I got lost and was getting a little scared. I didn't know anyone in this neighborhood who that I could ask for help and I was going to be late getting home. I saw a man working on a car. He could see that I was near tears and it was getting dark. He volunteered to take me home and somehow found my house with little help or good information from me. I sincerely thanked him repeatedly for saving my life, he just smiled.

At home, my family was just sitting down for dinner, so I wasn't in trouble. In the weeks to come, the tension in the house was to grow even more than usual because of the new house payment and the furniture that my parents had bought on credit. Now all the bills were starting to come in. That meant Dad had to work longer hours and go out of town more. Since Mom didn't do well under pressure, this just kept her mad all the time. Dad started to drink, and that made coming home scary as hell.

As usual, Tommy and I stayed out of the house as much as possible, and we learned all about our new neighborhood very quickly. We found the empty fields and a sandpit with cliffs in it that was a pretty cool place to hang out.

At first we hung out there together, but as we met more new kids, Tommy made friends quickly, I saw him less and less. After a while I only saw him at dinnertime. I had a few friends, so Tommy's absence from my life didn't bother me much.

Denny and I had become best friends I really liked going over to his house. After school one day, I asked if I could come over, but he said he had to go to a dentist appointment.

"Better you than me," was my reply. I smiled and walked away.

I wasn't going home, that would be a death wish. After the school bell rang, I headed to the local stores to kill some time. I had weird filling someone was watching me, I stopped and looked around and didn't notice anyone particular.

As I walked a little further up the road, the feeling made sense to me. I saw Brian's car and started smiling as I hurried up to it.

He yelled out the window, "Get in."

I jumped in the passenger seat and gave him a big hug around his neck. He didn't hug me back.

I sat back in my seat and asked, "How did you find me?"

"Your school sent a request for your transcripts."

I could tell he wasn't very happy and asked, "Brian, what's wrong?"

"I've been going through hell with all the guys asking about you. Each of them is trying to get information about you. They've been putting a lot of pressure on me. Roger and Carlos are madder than hell that I didn't confide in them. And to top it all off, Timmy, there was a party on Saturday. The guys made it a movie night, just for me, and who do you think was the star of the movie?"

I looked down at the floor and shrugged my shoulders. There was no way I could look him in the eye right now. I got nervous and scared when I saw where this was going.

Brian yelled, "Bullshit! Timmy, answer me! Who was the star?"

I just sat there quietly, shaking, and the tears I was trying to hold back slipped down my cheek.

Brian kept yelling his questions at me. "Who was it, Timmy? Say it! Say it!"

I used all my strength and said, "Me. It was me." How was I ever going to explain to him how they had forced me?

He was pissed by now, and his voice showed it, "That's right! How do you think it made me feel to find out that everyone knew about your movie career but me? I thought we told each other everything. I could have protected you." By then we were at his house pulling into the driveway.

He got out of the car and walked around to my door and opened it. He grabbed my arm and said, "Get out!"

We walked into the room, and he pushed my shoulder and said, 'Sit down."

I did and began to plead, "Please, Brian."

"Please Brian, what? You had a life I knew nothing about. I thought I knew you."

"You do!"

"Why didn't you tell me?"

I was praying he would understand and believe me. "I was scared, Brian. They threatened to hurt me and to tell my parents. They were going to show my dad the pictures and the movie. I didn't know what to do." I finally looked him in the eye, begging him to believe me, tears running down my face.

He stared at me for a long moment and said, "Well, Timmy, you're back, and it's like you never left. But there will be a price for you to pay for this."

"What is it? "I don't know yet." Then he smiled and said, "I sure missed you, kid. I can't stay mad at you; you're just so damn cute. I think you've grown an inch or two, and your hair has grown back. Damn you're perfect." He went from being mad to normal so quickly that I had to catch up. Then he wiped the tears from my face and bent down and hugged me and said, "I sure missed you."

I hugged him back tightly, afraid that I had lost this side of Brian.

He led me to his room like I had forgotten the way. We undressed and took a shower; the routine was like a hundred other times. He washed my hair and body, and I got out and dried while he finished washing. I fixed my hair and went to the bed and waited for him. He dried off and wrapped the towel around his waist and said to me, "Not here, Timmy." I looked up at him, confused, and he motioned for me to follow him. He gave no more explanation or reasons, and I was clueless as to what was happening.

As soon as I realized we were walking to the garage, I got nervous and asked, "What's going on Brian?"

He answered in a voice edged with evil intent, "Oh, have I got a surprise for you!"

He swung the door open, and I froze at the sight! This couldn't be happening. Brian had to know what fear and pain this had brought me before. This was used by people who hated me, not by someone who said he loved me. I was frozen in place. and somewhere in the back of my mind I could hear Brian talking to me. He said, "Rick and Todd let me borrow this. I believe they refer to it as a 'torture rack.'"

I turned to run, and he grabbed my arm, feeling my body tremble horribly. He continued, "Rick and Todd told me you love the rack, and after watching their home movies, I have to agree."

I begged and pleaded, pulling against his grip, "Please, Brian, no!"

He was staring at me, but his face was expressionless, and my feelings meant nothing to him. "You better not cry, Timmy! You did this for them, and you will do it for me."

He led me, my body still trembling because of past horrifying experiences with this torture rack, and buckled my arms and legs down. He even had his own movie camera set up. After he turned the camera on he picked up a whip, another item borrowed from Rick and Todd. Seeing that brought back my worst fears, and by now, I am losing it mentally. He walked behind me, and I held my breath, waiting for the pain. He lifted it up, and though he hit me lightly, I still flinched. I thought he was just teasing me and braced for the worst. None of the hits after that hurt any worse. I think he had planned to drag it out and make me really pay. But this was nothing compared to the torture that others had really inflicted on me.

This only hurt me because Brian wanted revenge and didn't understand why I had never told him about the movies. I only wished he could have seen it from my point of view. I never did it because I wanted to. I was forced to, and Rick and Todd scared me into silence.

Brian did not last very long, his excitement overcame him. He came up behind me, and I felt the pain as he entered. Normally Brian had self-control, but not this time. Seconds later, he was done. Then he lay on top of me breathing hard. The rack hurt my body already, and with Brian's weight added to it, I was having trouble breathing. I told him, and he got off me.

"You drive me crazy, Timmy," Brian whispered. He unbuckled my arms and legs and carried me back to the bedroom. We lay down and he wrapped his body around me, and we both fell asleep. This was the gentle side of Brian that I had missed so much. A few hours later, we got up, and Brian said, "I'd better take you home."

We were quiet at first in the car, and then he said, "I'll pick you up on Saturday at 8:00 in the morning at the Thrifty's store."

"Really But there isn't a party."

He smiled at me and replied, "I know."

I got my hopes up for the old times we'd had together.

"Can I spend the night?'

"How are you going to do it this time?"

"I will ask to spend the night at Denny's house; he is my new friend at this school."

"That would be great, Timmy."

He dropped me off a couple of blocks from my house. Dad was out of town, and Mom didn't cook much when he was gone. Even though it was late, it might work out. I stopped at the door and listened. I opened it slowly and listened. All was quiet.

Just as I stepped in the house, Tommy jumped out from behind the door and grabbed me, scaring me to death. I yelled and then caught myself, looking for Mom right away. I asked, "Where's Mom?"

Tommy answered, "She's at Grandma's."

"Oh, thank God."

"You are really late. Mom left a note to fix our own dinners."

Together we walked in the kitchen to get dinner ready.

Mom came home later, and we kept our distance until we could tell what mood she was in. Surprisingly it was a good mood tonight. She was a lot of fun when she was in a good mood. The problem was that you never knew which mood she would be in and how long it would last. That night, she wanted us to stay up and watch a movie with her. This gave me the right opportunity to ask about spending Saturday night at Denny's house. Since she was happy, she agreed to it.

I had no idea what I was in for on Saturday. I just knew Brian wanted me back. That made me feel better I thought things would go back to being like they'd been before. I had only been gone a month. What could have changed? But I was to find out that things would never be the same again.

On Saturday, I woke up early and quietly left the house. The walk to Thrifty's would take about twenty-five minutes, and I was thinking of my friends. I was hoping I would see Carlos and maybe Troy too. Carlos was older than me and watched over me like a big brother. Troy was two years older, but I felt like I was his big brother. We had all watched out for each other and had gotten close. I didn't have to wait too long for Brian too pulled up, and he had Roger and Carlos with him. Carlos gave me a big hug, and Roger surprised me with one too. Roger was Carlos's uncle and Brian's boyfriend, and he didn't like me before, so I was surprised at his friendliness. Brian was smiling as I got in the car, and I sat in the back with Carlos.

Carlos asked quietly so the guys in the front couldn't hear, "Where the hell you been?"

"We moved to Yorba Linda."

"Brian said you moved far away and wouldn't tell anyone where you were. Rick and Todd were going to hire a private investigator to find you. At the party Saturday, Rick and Todd showed their home movies of you. By the way, you are quite the actor, aren't you? Brian went ballistic, and no one could settle him down. Now he has found you, and you're in trouble. What's going on?"

I explained as best I could, "I just did what Brian told me to do."

Carlos kept interrogating me, "Did Brian tell you to make the movies too?"

I bowed my head, wishing he could understand my point of view, "No, Carlos, he didn't. But it's not my fault!"

"Oh really; you didn't tell Brian or me. We could have helped you. You shouldn't have kept a secret like that from Brian." I could tell that was all he was going to say or even try to understand on the subject, so I just kept quiet and looked out the window.

When Brian stopped in front of an iron double gate, I had no problem recognizing this specific mansion. This man, I did not know his name, had been very cruel to me in the past. By the comments Brian and Roger were making in the front seat, I could tell he was a main player in their group now. In the past, Brian and Roger had been the only leaders and I could tell this was changing. Today was going downhill really fast for me I nervously asked Brian, "What are we doing here?"

Brian answered sarcastically, "Not we, Timmy, just you."

I was upset with this answer, "No, Brian, please. This guy hates me."

Brian answered, "You think everyone hates you. Get over it."

I stammered, "You're wrong."

"I told you there was a price to be paid; this is the beginning of it."

I begged, "Please, Brian, don't leave me with this guy."

"It's not 'this guy.' He has a name; it's Bill. And you will be just fine. Now get out of the car and get your ass in that house."

I opened the door and got out. I walked slowly toward the house like I was going to my own execution. I turned to look at Brian, my expression pleading for mercy from him; instead he just waved me on. I knocked on the door, and to my surprise, a teenage boy answered it. He was around fourteen or fifteen and was tall and slender with dark brown hair and dark eyes. He asked, "Can I help you?"

"Is your dad home? Oh, you must be Timmy. Come on in." I turned around when I heard Brian's car pulling out of the driveway.

I walked in the house and the boy told me, "Dad is getting dressed. Do you want to go check out the game room?" He obviously had no idea that I had been there before. This was a place used frequently to do the guys monthly parties.

"Sure, that would be great."

He was real proud of his house, and I could understand why because it was a mansion. He pointed things out as we walked down the hall. Finally we got to the playroom, which was absolutely huge and had a bowling alley attached to it. There was no need to tell him I had seen it before—especially because I didn't want to have to explain a side of his father that he apparently was unaware of. I didn't think he could handle the truth—if I had said something like, *about six months ago, your dad and a group of horny men played out their fantasies and tied me to a cross. And a month later he strapped me to a rack and beat the hell out of me. Yeah, your dad is a real peach.*

He said, "Let's play air hockey."

"What's your name?"

"Tyler."

We played a couple games, and it was like playing against a pro.

He asked me, "Do you like bowling?"

I answered honestly, "I don't know. I've never bowled before."

He taught me the basics and I was starting to enjoy the game. We played for over an hour, and I almost forgot why I was even there. I had no instructions, so I didn't know what to expect. I just knew it wouldn't be good because this man could be cruel. My worst nightmares came true with him.

Bill walked in and called my name. It startled me. I quit playing and walked over and stood in front of him, "Sir?"

He said, "Come with me. Tyler, go to your room."

I followed him to his office. I was so nervous my mouth was dry, and I felt light-headed.

Bill could see how scared I was and said, "Just relax, Timmy. Do you know why you are here?"

I swallowed and answered, "No."

"Well I'll tell you. You're going to help me with my son. When you got here, he wasn't supposed to play games with you. He was supposed to seduce you into having sex with him. But after an hour of bowling, I realized he had lost his nerve."

I thought this guy was really sick. I didn't know what to say.

He saw the confusion on my face and said, "You don't have to understand. Just do as I say. I still have the whip, and you know I know how to use it." He saw the fear on my face and that made him feel better; it reassured him of the control he still had over me.

He led me upstairs to a huge bedroom. It had its own living room area with a couch and loveseat, a TV, and a big fireplace with a sheepskin rug on the floor and a huge bathroom.

Bill looked at me and said, "Take your clothes off."

I immediately feel embarrassed, and he read it on my face.

He said, "Knock it off! Just take off your clothes now!"

I took off my shirt and looked at him; his impatience showed in his face. I took off my shoes and socks and looked again. He snaps his fingers and said, "Now, your pants and underwear." He gathered my clothes and told me to sit on the couch and walked out the door.

I sat there feeling really stupid and uncomfortable. A few minutes later, Bill walked in with Tyler, and he was naked too. Tyler's face was bright red, and he was dying of embarrassment too. Bill didn't say anything; he just turned around and walked out the door. Tyler walked over to me and his hands were covering his privates. He walked into the bathroom and grabbed a towel and wrapped it around him. He came back over to the couch and stood staring at me. Of course he didn't bring a towel for me. Now I was the only one not covered, and I didn't know what was expected of me.

So I asked, "Am I here because your dad wanted you to do this or because you want to do this?"

"Both. Dad showed me a movie with you in it."

Before he could finish I said, "No shit!" and my face turned red.

"Are you embarrassed?"

"Yeah, I am."

He smiled and asked, "Now what?"

I stood up and said, "Come with me."

When it was over and Tyler was leaving the room, I asked him if he would please bring me my clothes. I waited a long time, and finally Bill came through the door saying, "What did you do to my son?!"

I sat up quickly, afraid I was in a lot of trouble. Then he smiled and laughed at me, and I asked, "So can I get dressed now?"

"No, not until you put a grin on my face too." Then he turned and shut the door.

It was around noon when he was done with me and I could finally get dressed. I went downstairs and Tyler was waiting for me.

He asked, "Timmy, do you want to play in the game room with me."

"Sure. But can I have something to eat first?"

He nodded his head yes and walked me to the kitchen. It looked like a kitchen you would see in a restaurant. These people went overboard in everything.

Tyler asked, "What do you want?"

"I'm so hungry it doesn't matter."

He fixed me a roast beef sandwich, and it tasted really good.

Bill walked in and said, "I called Brian, and he will be here in about an hour." Then he handed me an envelope and said, "That's for you. I wasn't going to pay you after that last stunt you pulled, trying to leave the group like that. But Tyler insisted, so I agreed. Now I know it wasn't your fault."

Tyler smiled real big after Bill said that.

I put the envelope in my pocket and Bill asked, "Aren't you going to count it?"

"No. I know it will be more than enough."

Bill looked me in the eye and said, "Timmy, that money is for you, not Brian."

I nodded in agreement. When I was done eating, Tyler and I went back to the playroom. We weren't down there long when Carlos came walking in.

Carlos asks, "What are you guys up to?"

I said, "Hey, Carlos. This is Tyler."

They shook hands.

"We are playing air hockey. Do you want to play?"

"We can't. We have to go."

Tyler looked disappointed as Carlos left the room.

Tyler asked me, "Timmy, will you come back?"

"Yes"

"Can I have your phone number?"

I didn't know if that was allowed within the group or not so I told him, "Yeah, but don't tell anyone you have it. Okay?" He nodded his head.

Brian and Roger were waiting in the car, and I headed for the front door to leave.

Bill stopped me at the door and said, "Timmy, you don't have to be afraid of me. Okay?"

Somehow I felt like I could believe him, and I smiled and nodded yes and went outside. I ran to catch up to Carlos and jumped on his back. He laughed and gave me a piggyback ride to the car. We got into the backseat, and Brian pulled out of the driveway.

Brian asked, "So how did it go?"

"Fine"

"Are you mad at me?"

I really wasn't, but I didn't want Brian to get off that easy. I answered, "A little."

We drove in silence until we pulled in the driveway, and Brian told me, "There is a surprise in your room."

At my age that got my attention real quick.

I replied quickly, "Yeah"

I ran to the front door waiting for him to open it.

I was surprised to find my room the same way I left it. I had thought Brian would have a new kid from his class already.

My surprise wasn't a new toy. It was even better. Troy was waiting for me! Troy was playing with my race car set and turned around when I yelled his name. He said, "Timmy, it's you!"

"Yeah, who else would it be?" He ran over to me and hugged me.

"Where have you been?" He stepped back and looked at me. Even though he was a couple of years older than me and a couple of inches taller, we still looked eye to eye, well kind of. It was probably my imagination.

He had tears, and I asked, "Troy what's wrong?"

He replied honestly, "I thought you were dead."

"Why would you think that?"

"You were here one day and gone the next. I thought they killed you."

"Who are you talking about?"

"Any of them" Rick Todd, anyone from the group" Things were getting really weird. I didn't think anyone could leave the group. Where were you?"

"I moved."

"That's what they told us, but I didn't believe them. If you moved, then why are you back now?

"They found me."

"Really'

"how?

"I think because they had to send paperwork to my new school. I'm not really sure."

"Are you in trouble? Are they going to punish you?"

"Probably"

"Are you sorry they found you?"

I stopped and thought about how to answer that. I didn't miss the pain and humiliation. I didn't miss not knowing what each party or group activity held for me. I did miss Brian and hanging out at his house. I really missed the boys that I had become so close to. We lived in a secret world that we could only share with each other. And that world made me feel important.

I answered, "No, I missed you guys."

"They showed some of our movies at the last party."

I looked away, "Yeah, I heard."

"Some of the guys threatened Brian if he didn't bring you back "That really surprised me.

Troy had changed a lot since I'd first met him. He used to be wild and cocky and not have a care in the world. Then he begged to join the group, and all that changed. Now he looked beaten down and very unsure of himself As if he had been deflated from the inside out. I put my hand on his shoulder and looked deep into his eyes so I could see the truth and asked, "Troy, are you all right?"

He took a deep breath and answered, "Yeah, now that you're back it will be all right. I won't feel so alone."

"What about Carlos and Nick. Weren't they around?"

"It's just not the same. Just promise me you won't leave like that again."

I smiled and answered, "Okay, I promise." It was funny because this made me feel older and stronger and like I had more control over what happened than he did. But he was wrong; I was scared a lot of the time also. The only ones who had control were the adults, and we kids were never going to be able to understand them.

"Timmy, did you know Brian has the rack in his garage now?"

I nodded my head and answered, "Yeah, I know."

Troy asked, "Is that for you?"

I nodded again.

Troy said, "Oh shit!"

Then Carlos walked in and asked, "What are you guys talking about?" Before either of us could answer Carlos added, "See, Troy, I told you they didn't kill him." He looked at me and asked, "Did Troy tell you that he was scared?"

I smiled and answered, "Yeah." Then we all laughed.

But inside I was scared. I had been scared to leave, and I would always wonder if coming back was going to be dangerous for me. It was easier to just block it all out, and that is what I did best. So I put those thoughts away and enjoyed being around my friends again.

Carlos said, "Brian told me to come and get you. He is in his room with Roger."

I opened the door to the bedroom, and Brian and Roger were laying there talking. I ran over to the bed and jumped on it and attacked Brian, hoping for a good wrestling match, and found him up for it. We wrestled for a few minutes and then he finally just pinned me. To my surprise, Roger joined in to help, and they both tickled me until I gave in. I had held out a long time though. Brian said, "That's why I love you, kid."

After they let me up, Brian asked, "So, Timmy, what really happened at Bill's house?"

"Why?"

"We just want to know."

So I began to tell the story, "His son, Tyler, was there, and he let me in, and we went to the playroom and hung out for about an hour or so. Bill came and got me, and we went to his office. He told me that Tyler was supposed to seduce me, whatever that means. I was being vague and skipping parts, and Brian knew that.

Brian stopped me and said, "You tell me everything. Don't leave anything out."

It was really embarrassing to have to tell the details, but I did. Then I reached in my pocket and pulled out an envelope that Bill gave me. I said bravely, "He told me that it's for me, not you Brian."

This made him mad, and he said, "Give it here!"

I handed it to him and asked, "How much is there?" I hadn't counted it yet.

Brian and Roger counted it for me and were very surprised.

Anxiously I asked, "How much?"

Brian answered, "You must have been really good."

"Well, how much?"

Brian just folded the envelope and put it in his pocket, and Roger said, "It's your night, Timmy. What do you want to do?"

I thought about it and answered, "Just hang out with you guys." What I really meant was time with Brian by himself, but that wasn't going to happen. They called for Carlos and Troy, and we all decided on dinner and a movie.

Brian announced, "Timmy is paying for everyone tonight."

We all laughed. I didn't care about paying, but I was dying to know how much was in the envelope.

Brian told us all to dress up. Troy didn't have any nice clothes with him, but I still had a closetful in my room. Carlos helped us pick out what to wear. He had been the one to help me buy all my clothes. Soon enough, the three of us were done and looking really sharp. It was great, just like we were the three musketeers.

We went to dinner at a really nice restaurant. We laughed and joked and had a great time. At times, we were just plain silly, but Brian and Roger were good sports about it. As a matter of fact, they laughed with us most of the time. Troy finally started acting like his old self, and that gave me hope. We went to the movies, and I got to sit between Carlos and Troy. I kept flicking popcorn seeds across the theater, sometimes hitting people in the head. No one could figure out who was doing it. Carlos and Troy did their best to keep a straight face, but Brian figured it out and made me stop.

After the movies, we went back to Roger's house. We went straight to Carlos's room and hung out. Carlos fell asleep around midnight in his bed, and Troy and I were on a roll away.

"Thanks," Troy said to me.

"For what"

"For making tonight so much fun"

"I think we all had a little bit to do with that."

Troy quickly answered, "No, you're wrong. When I'm with Carlos and Nick, we don't have fun, especially normal fun like tonight."

I smiled and said thanks, and we both fell asleep. In the morning before we could even wake up, Troy's dad came to get him. Carlos tried to wake up Troy without bothering me, but I woke up. Troy begged and pleaded to stay but his dad, Richard, insisted that they go. Troy came back upstairs to tell us good-bye.

Carlos came and sat next to me and asked, "Are you sad they found you?"

It was funny that the other kids involved kept asking this. I answered, "No."

"Why?"

I wasn't sure how to explain. "I don't know."

"Why didn't you tell me that you were moving?"

"Brian told me not to."

"Why didn't you tell me about the home movies?"

"Carlos," I turned to look at his face, "I was really scared of them."

He kept pressing. "Too scared to tell Brian or Roger?"

I surprised Carlos with my answer. "Roger already knew."

Shocked, he asked, "Are you kidding?!"

"No. He was at a few of them."

"Did you tell Brian?"

Surprised he'd even asked me, I answered, "No way."

He was kind of frantic and said, "Don't ever tell him, okay. You have to promise." He jumped on me and pinned me to the bed and said, "Timmy, you have to swear you won't say anything to Brian."

I decided to tease him and answered lightly, "Sure, whatever you say."

This made him mad, and he said, "Bullshit, Timmy! You have to swear!"

I laughed to let him know I was only joking, but he wasn't laughing with me. He hit me on the chest—not too hard, just hard enough to get my attention. I told him, "Look, Carlos, I haven't told yet. You know I won't tell."

"Just swear."

"Okay, I swear."

He still didn't get off me. He was staring at me, and I stared back. Then he surprised me with, "You know, those movies turned out pretty good. I want to be in the next one with you."

I quickly answered, "No, you don't."

"Yes, I do. Would you rather have Nick instead of me?"

"No. I would rather not do it at all. Now please get off me."

Carlos was feeling the power now, "You don't have a choice now do you?"

"No, I don't. Why are you being so mean to me, Carlos?" I pleaded.

He chuckled, "I'm not."

"Then get off me!"

Finally he did, but he let me know it was his choice.

"Don't you get it, Timmy?' Carlos asked.

I felt like I was in the dark again in this conversation. "Get what?"

Carlos explained, "I didn't know Roger had anything to do with those movies. If Brian finds out, there will be hell to pay. I'm with Roger, and you're with Brian, and they can keep us apart."

"Carlos, I wasn't going to tell anyway. Don't worry."

Carlos reached out and grabbed my hand and pulled me to my feet and said, "Okay, let's get ready."

Carlos didn't have a bashful bone in his body. He was Puerto Rican and always had a nice tan. He had dark, wavy hair; dark eyes; and a great body. He had a natural build and took time to make it even better by working out. After all we'd been through; I was comfortable enough to undress in front of him too. I looked over at him and giggled. This was one of the most stupid things I could have done. I was no match for Carlos's strength. I was only ten years old and had sandy blond hair and a slender build.

Carlos pushed me and tripped me at the same time. I fall hard on my butt, and he jumped on me pinning my arms down with his knees. He moved was so fast, I didn't even see it coming. He punched me in the chest then jumps up and slammed himself down on my stomach, and it knocked the wind out of me. Even though I was struggling for every breath, he did it all one more time. I burst out crying, and he slaps my face. He yelled, "What do you think is so funny?"

I was still trying to catch my breath and couldn't even answer him.

Seeing how hard I was crying, he stopped hitting me. He didn't let me up yet, but he let me catch my breath. He yelled again, "What the hell do you think is so funny?"

I finally found my voice and answered, "Nothing. It's just that Roger makes you shave and I know you hate it."

Just hearing me say it made him even madder, and he started hitting me all over again. He finally got off me, and I rolled onto my side and couldn't stop crying.

He said disgustedly, "Suck it up, Timmy. You're fine! Don't ever laugh at me again," he added with authority.

I struggled to talk and tell him I was sorry. He helped me off the floor, and I stood there like a whipped puppy. Finally he made me look him in the eye, and I saw compassion for the first time. "Carlos, apologized"

Then Carlos explained why he reacted like that. "I don't like to be laughed at"

It's so embarrassing having to shave that I can't even get undressed for PE at school. That was my favorite class. I'm really good at sports. Rick gave me a doctor's excuse, and now I have to go to health class. It sucks!" I just stood there and listened. He kept on, "Timmy, you can't stay young forever. Everyone has to grow up."

After we showered and went back to the bedroom, I could see what Carlos wanted to do. I started to get dressed and he said, "Not yet." He got a brush and fixed my hair. I swear it was as if everyone went to the same school. Roger probably had been doing this to Carlos for years. And it was the same thing that Brian did to me. My mind was spinning from the ass whipping that Carlos had given me, and I knew this was his strange way of making it up to me.

I said, "Carlos, no!"

Then he pushed me on the bed and pinned me for the third time that day. He could see the fear in my eyes and said, "I'm not going to hurt you." Then he kissed my cheek and stroked my hair and asked, "Are you still mad at me?"

I nodded my head yes.

He asked, "How long are you going to be mad?"

I just shrugged my shoulders for an answer.

He looked at me for a moment and then, to my surprise, grabbed my privates and threatened me, "You aren't ever going to laugh at me again, are you?!"

I jumped and said quickly, "No, Carlos!"

He laughed at me and let go. Then he proceeded to get his pleasure. I felt violated and very sad that this whole morning had turned out so bad.

I could smell breakfast cooking and realized just how hungry I was. Brian and Roger were almost done, and Brian asked, "Are you guys hungry?"

Carlos answered for both of us, "Yes."

We all sat down. Brian could see something was wrong by the look on my face. "What's wrong with you?" he asked.

Carlos quickly answered for me. "Just a little misunderstanding he'll be all right."

Roger asked Carlos to explain, and Carlos answered, "We worked it out, right, Timmy?"

I wanted this over with, so I put a smile on my face and answered, "Yes."

Brian told me after breakfast that he was taking me home. I begged to stay. "But it's still early."

He answered, "Sorry, buddy. I've got some things to do."

"Can't I go with you?"

"Not today."

I ate the rest of my breakfast, trying to hide my disappointment. When I was done eating, I left to get my stuff together. Carlos was disappointed and asked Brian, "Why can't Timmy stay here with us? We can take him home later."

Brian got mad and said, "No. Just leave it alone, Carlos."

In the car, Brian told me that, on Thursday, Roger would pick me up at the shopping center near my house. I nodded in agreement.

"Why were you upset at breakfast?" Brian asked.

"Carlos."

He wanted a complete answer. "What about Carlos?"

So I told the story. "Carlos beat me up because I laughed at him. Roger makes him shave, and he is really embarrassed about it."

Brian chuckled. "You really laughed at him, huh? I would have kicked your ass too."

That's not what I wanted to hear. "So you're on his side?"

"Timmy, if that's what happened, I agree with Carlos." I just sat looking out the window real quiet. Brian finished, "Now you're mad at me too."

"No. It's just been a tough morning. It's only 10:00 am. Do you really have to take me home?"

"Yeah, Timmy, I do."

He pulled into the Thrifty Shopping Center, and before I got out, I asked, "Brian, I don't have any money. Could you give me some, please?"

He pulled out his wallet and gave me forty dollars.

"Is that enough?"

I smiled and said, "Yes."

I started to walk home and realized how stupid that would be. I changed directions and went to Denny's house. Last week, Denny's mom had met my mom, and ever since then, she had been kind of cold to me. Mom had that effect on people. It really upset me because Denny was a cool kid and a good friend. I knocked on the door, and Mrs. Ross answered.

Before I could ask, she told me, "Denny can't come out and play."

I just nodded. I wasn't surprised. I turned and started my long walk home.

I listened at the door and everything was quiet, but I still walked in, staying alert to any sound. My brother was in the living room watching TV.

I asked "Where's Mom?"

"She's still in bed. She's sick." Tommy replied. "Did you have fun at Denny's?"

"Yeah, it was great."

"Who's Tyler?"

(Oh shit)

I thought "Just a kid I know."

"Well that kid called about five times already, and I'm sick of it. You better call him back before he wakes mom up."

"I don't have his number."

Tommy handed me a piece of paper with Tyler's number on it. All I could think was that I could be in big trouble if Tyler's dad answered the phone. I figured I could always hang up if that happened. But I got lucky and Tyler answered the phone.

"Hey, Tyler, what's up?"

"I've been trying to call you."

"I know. My brother just told me."

"I'm having a party on Saturday night. Do you want to come?"

"Your dad would never let me come."

"Yes he will."

"Did you ask him?"

"No not yet."

"I'm telling you right now, he'll say no. Why do you want me to come?"

"We're friends, aren't we?"

"Yeah," I answered, but I was thinking that we were from totally different worlds. I'm just the hired boy who doesn't have a choice. You're the rich kid who got everything he wanted, including me. "How many people are going to be there?"

"Lots"

"Look, Tyler, your fifteen years old, and I'm almost eleven. Your high school friends aren't going to want me hanging around."

"Do you want to come or not?" Tyler asked. I could tell his feelings were getting hurt.

"I do, but your dad won't let you invite me."

"He won't even be there."

"Still, without his permission, I won't come."

"Okay, I will get it and call you right back."

"Tyler, don't call, my mother is asleep. I'll call you back in thirty minutes."

"Okay, don't forget."

I went to my bedroom and lay down. I was only going to lay there for a minute but I fell asleep. I woke to my brother hitting me and saying, "Wake up, asshole! You better hope your friend didn't wake Mom up!"

I had fallen into a deep sleep, and it took a minute for his words to sink in. Tommy said one more time, "The phone is for you!"

I stumbled to the living room and picked up the phone, "Hello."

"Hey, Timmy, you said you'd call me back."

"I'm sorry. I fell asleep."

"My dad said you could come."

I was silent and in shock because I thought there was no way Tyler's dad would want me at Tyler's party. Because I was silent for so long, Tyler put his dad on the phone.

"Timmy, how did Tyler get your phone number?"

I was in trouble now! "Tyler asked me for it. I'm sorry, sir. I shouldn't have given it to him. Please tell Tyler this has all been a big mistake."

"Wait a minute, Timmy." He could hear the anxiety in my voice. "I'm just kidding. What was the last thing I told you yesterday?"

I thought for a second and then said, "I don't have to be afraid of you."

"Right If Tyler wants you at his party, then its fine with me. But no funny business" Do you know what I mean by that?"

"Yes sir. You want everyone to keep their clothes on."

"Damn, Timmy, you're smart. But it's a pool party, so bathing suits are acceptable. But you have the right idea." Then he handed the phone back to Tyler.

Tyler said, "See I told you he would say yes. It starts at 6:00 pm. on Saturday."

"Where do you live?"

"You've been over here before."

"Yeah, I know, but I didn't pay any attention sitting in the back seat."

"I live in Yorba Linda."

"So do I. I thought it was close."

It wasn't easy, but I finally figured out where Tyler lived. I knew I could ride my bike there, even though it was hard riding up those hills.

Monday at school was an ordinary day, and Denny asked if I would walk home with him. I noticed he hadn't asked me to stay and play at his house, just to walk him home.

Since I had the chance, I asked Denny, "Your mom doesn't like me does she?"

"I don't think it's you."

"Then who"

"Your mom"

"So why do you want me to walk you home?"

"David and a couple of his friends want to beat me up."

"Do you mean David, the big kid at recess?"

"Yes!"

"Shit, Denny, he can kick both our asses." I could tell how scared he was and offered, "Call your mom and have her pick you up."

"She won't."

"Why?"

"My dad wants me to face my fears."

"Did you tell him how big this guy is?"

"Yeah, he thinks I'm exaggerating."

"Wow, Denny, and your parents think my mom is nuts." Then we both laughed. "It sucks to be you." I was kind of joking and kind of meant it.

"Will you walk me home?"

"No."

"You don't have to fight. Just after he beats me up, make sure I get home."

I thought, *Hell, I'll see a good fight.* Then I thought, *No, he's too scared. He'll never fight back.*

"Yeah, I'll walk you home."

The final bell rang, and school was out. I didn't have to look for Denny. He sat in the desk ahead of me. He was so scared I felt I needed to encourage him. "Look, Denny, don't worry. We'll get out of this." I didn't know how I was going to do this, but I felt like I wanted to protect him.

As we walked to his house, we found David and his goons waiting for us. They walked toward us, and the group made a circle around us. David looked at me. "Are you here to watch or get your ass kicked?"

I don't know what made me say it, and I couldn't believe it was coming out of my mouth, "No, you chicken shit. I'm here to kick your ass." Then I raised my fist. Instead of hitting him, I snap kicked him right in the balls. He fell forward and I snap kicked him in the face. He fell crying, and his friends ran off.

Denny was just standing there with his mouth open.

I grabbed him and said, "Let's get out of here." And we ran to his house.

When we reached his driveway, he stopped. "I thought you were just going to watch?" His tone was a question.

"I know, but from where I come from, these guys are a dime a dozen. Hey, he doesn't have an older brother, does he?"

"I don't think so."

"Good. Well, Denny, I got to go before those guys regroup."

I left and went back by the place where I'd beaten David up, and he was still lying there crying. I felt kind of sorry for him because I had been where he was at many times. I laughed inside because I knew the karate classes Brian and I had gone to had really paid off. I asked David, "Are you all right?"

He looked up at me, and I could tell he was really messed up. It was cold out, but I took off my shirt and told him to lie on his back. He was scared of me, and I reassured him I wouldn't hurt him. I put my shirt over his nose to stop the bleeding. He tried to sit up but I stopped him, telling him, "Not until you stop bleeding."

He lay there quietly for a few minutes and let me help him. I felt sorry for him. But I knew that, if he had won, I would be lying in the same spot and no one would be helping me out. Nevertheless, I couldn't be like that, I couldn't ignore someone in pain. I moved the shirt away from his face, and I could see that the bleeding had stopped, but he was a mess.

Then to my surprise, Denny and his mom pulled up in a car and she asked, "Is he okay?"

"No. He's hurt pretty badly."

Mrs. Ross got out of the car and helped me get David to his feet. We got him in the backseat, and she told me and Denny to go straight back to their house, adding that Denny should get a shirt for me to wear.

We ran back to Denny's house, and Mrs. Ross took David to his house.

When we got inside, Denny told me, "I think my mom likes you again."

I smiled at him. We went to his room, and I got a shirt to wear. We waited downstairs until Mrs. Ross got home. It seemed to take forever, but it was probably only twenty minutes.

She walked in the door and didn't say anything to either one of us. After a moment, she flopped down on the couch and asked me, "Timmy, did you have to hit him so hard?"

"Mrs. Ross, did you see how big he was?"

She smiled and answered, "Yes, but he's a big baby. He cried all the way home."

Denny and I looked at each other and laughed.

"Timmy, would you like to eat dinner with us tonight?"

I smiled and nodded my head.

"You better call your parents then."

"It will be okay with them."

"Call them anyways."

To my surprise, Dad answered the phone. "Dad it's you."

"Okay, so it is."

"Can I eat dinner over at Denny's house?"

"Did you know your mother is sick?"

"Yes. Do you want me to come home?" There was silence on the phone because Dad wasn't used to making these kinds of decisions.

"No. You can stay for dinner."

I thanked him and hung up. Denny and I went up to his room to play for about an hour. Mrs. Ross called us for dinner, and when I sat down at the table, she introduced me to her husband.

"It's nice to meet you, Timmy," he said.

I reached out and shook his hand.

When everyone was seated, they all held hands and Denny's dad said a prayer. What really surprised me was that they prayed specifically for David, the kid I had just beaten up.

Mr. Ross was not very tall, and he was dressed in a suit and tie. I figured he worked in an office. He had dark hair and blue eyes and a great sense of humor. I caught his wife rolling her eyes a few times at his jokes. He also thanked me for sticking up for Denny. After dinner, I thanked them and told them it was time for me to go home. Mrs. Ross offered me a ride home, but I assured her I had no problem walking home.

Things were different at home right now. Dad was gone a lot taking any job he could get to make money, even if it was far away.

Mom was sick all the time and didn't have the energy to stay on top of me and my brother. This left us with even more freedom. Sometimes we didn't come home until 9:00 or 10:00 at night.

Mom was still out of control when she was mad. She never needed a good reason to go off on you; she just had to think you did something against her. Then you would get the hell beaten out of you. You get the point; she really didn't need a reason, so why have a bunch of rules. Why set up a system of rules and punishments when punishment was arbitrary? We knew to keep our rooms and the bathroom clean. If Mom left us a list of chores, whoever was home would get it done.

When I got home that night, Mom and Dad were lying on the couch watching TV.

I said, "Hi, I'm home."

"Tyler called for you, and he wants you to call him back," Dad said.

"Thanks, Dad."

We had three phones—one in the living room, one in the kitchen, and one in my parent's bedroom. I used the one in the kitchen.

Tyler answered the phone. "Hello."

"Hey, it's me, Timmy."

"Do you want to come over after school tomorrow?"

"Are you sure it's all right?"

"Dad will be gone until Thursday. He wouldn't mind anyways."

"Okay, I'll see you tomorrow." I figured I might as well make a practice run to his house on my bike and see if I knew the way.

After I hung up, I went to my room and got ready for bed. I had forgotten all about David and the fight already, even though Dad would have liked the story.

The next day, it was all around school; everyone was talking about it, even the teachers. Other kids were congratulating me, even ones I had never met before. After I sat down at my desk, Ms. Right received a message summoning me to the principal's office. On my way to the office, I wondered how I could be in trouble. David and I had fought off school property.

I knocked on the door and was told to come in. The first thing I saw was David sitting in one of the chairs with two black eyes, a swollen nose, and a fat lip. I couldn't believe the damage I had done to him. I didn't have a scratch on me. Mr. Davies just looked at both of us. David started to speak, and our principal stopped him right away, saying, "You just shut your mouth!" He just continued to stare at us, and I felt like he was looking right through us.

Then to my surprise, Mr. Davies looked at David and laughed. "You've been walking around this school for five years scaring and beating up little kids half your size. You finally got what you deserve."

I couldn't believe it, but David actually started to cry.

Mr. Davies continued, "How many times have you told me that I couldn't do anything to you because it was off school property? Well this time, you're right. I can't help you. Timmy, go back to class."

I walked out and could still hear Mr. Davies laughing and saying, "You're telling me that little kid whipped your ass."

I smiled, and I looked up to see the office ladies stand and clap for me. They stopped me and congratulated me. I guess this kid had been terrorizing this whole school for years. I knew I had just been lucky, but no one else had to know that.

At lunch, David was treated as an outcast by everyone but his small group. They were still too scared of him not to be his friend. My table was overflowing with new friends.

David stood up and walked over to me. "Just wait, you little punk!" he said" Next time, you are going to get it"

"I was just playing with you this time. Next time I'm really going to hurt you." I saw the fear in his eyes and knew he would never fight me again. Losing to me had taken something out of him. He turned to walk away, his head and shoulders bowed ever so slightly. He wasn't sure of himself and cocky anymore.

I yelled, "Hey, David."

He stopped and turned. When he saw me coming, he flinched a little, thinking I was going to hit him. This was still ironic to me because he was so much bigger than me. He seemed at least a foot taller and outweighed me by fifty pounds.

I told him, "I don't want to fight you. Cant' we be friends?"

He was completely surprised and quickly said, "Yes."

We shook hands, and I invited him to come sit at my table. It was then that I noticed how quiet the cafeteria had become. David smiled and followed me.

I could see the horror on the faces of the kids sitting at the table. This guy had been terrorizing them, and they couldn't understand what was happening. I was supposed to be the new hero and protect them from him. Deep down I knew I had been lucky, and the next time would turn out a lot different for me. Plus, you never know when you'll need a really big kid on your side. I explained my thinking to my friends latter that day, and they agreed.

After lunch on the playground, David played a game of kickball with us and, for the first time, didn't pick a fight with anyone. It ended up being a great day at school.

After the bell rang, Denny asked if I was coming over, but I explained that I had other plans. He looked disappointed, and I told him I would see him tomorrow at school.

I rode my bike down the busy streets I had a long ride to get to Tyler's house. I wasn't quite halfway when it started to rain. There were some steep hills, and I had to push my bike up one of them. It took about an hour, and I was wet and cold all the way to my bones by the time I arrived.

I announced myself on the intercom at the end of the driveway, and Tyler answered and let me in.

Tyler laughed and asked, "What took you so long?" Before I could answer he said, "Timmy, you can't come in the house like that. My dad would kill us." He pointed to the garage and went to open the door. I rode my bike to the garage, which was on the back side of the house and realized there were six garage doors to choose from. When the door opened, it was unreal. It was like a large warehouse full of exotic cars. The floor was painted gray and shined like glass.

The cars were polished to perfection. I stood frozen to my spot, afraid I would dirty the garage floor.

"Come on in," Tyler said.

"I'll get the floor dirty."

"This is the garage. It will be okay."

I still took off my shoes before I walked in. Tyler threw me a towel, and I started drying my face. He walked over to a black Porsche 911 and stared at it. "This baby is going to be mine when I'm sixteen. At least I hope it will be."

"Wow! When will you be sixteen?"

"Next month."

He was older than I thought. We looked at the other cars. There were a Ferrari and a Maserati in the group, and I was very impressed. Then we walked to the door leading to the laundry room. Tyler said, "You're going to have to take those clothes off." I did and wrapped the towel around me. Tyler put my clothes in the dryer.

"Do you have something I can wear?"

"Yeah" He handed me a pair of sweat pants and a T-shirt. I realized how much bigger he was when I had to roll up the pant legs and the shirt hung so big on me.

Tyler laughed and said, "You look like a wet puppy."

"Thanks."

The laundry room was connected to a very large kitchen. A lady stood at the stove cooking. "This is Anna. She cooks and cleans for us."

"You must be Timmy. I have heard a lot about you."

This shocked me, since Tyler barely knew me. The only thing I was to Bill was Tyler's paid toy.

Anna who was from Mexico' walked over to me and pushed my wet hair away from my face and said in a Spanish accent, "You are a beautiful boy."

I smiled and thanked her.

"Oh and polite too"

Then she spoke in Spanish to Tyler.

Tyler asked quickly, "Do you understand Spanish?"

I shook my head no. Then they spoke for a few minutes and laughed.

"Timmy's clothes are in the dryer." Tyler said.

"I will take care of them."

I followed Tyler up the spiral staircase and down a hall to his room. I was completely blown away. It was nothing like Denny's room, It was huge" With A large TV and stereo and a fireplace made the room fill like you were in a fancy hotel. A small refrigerator was stocked with drinks and snacks. Tyler offered me a coke. It wasn't like a kid's room it had a teenage fill to it. A very large bathroom featured a sunken in tub and a separate shower. Tyler opened a safe in his closet and showed me his gold coin collection.

I asked, "Is it real gold?"

"Yeah, it's real gold. And it's worth a lot."

"Is this your collection or your dad's?"

"This is mine. Dad helps me collect the coins."

"So they are for both of you?"

"No Just mine. Dad has his own."

"What does your dad do?"

"I can't tell you."

"Why?"

"Because that's the one thing I promised my dad I wouldn't talk to you about."

I was intrigued how one family could have so much. I noticed that Tyler liked showing me his things; I think it made him feel superior to me. He liked to see the awe on my face because I had no idea how to comprehend this kind of wealth. We ended up in the game room, and he beat me at every game we played. He could see that I was getting tired of losing and started letting me win every now and then. All the while, I was wondering why he liked to hang out with me. I was five years younger than he was, and he had plenty of rich teenagers to hang out with.

"Follow me," Tyler said.

We took a long walk, and he opened a door up and showed me the gym. It wasn't like Brian's garage with its workout equipment. This was a full gym with all kinds of professional equipment. We walked through that room and entered the steam room with a Jacuzzi.

"Wow, Tyler, you have everything." I was so impressed.

Then Tyler started to undress. This shocked me because of how bashful he was last weekend. He got in the Jacuzzi and motions for me to come in too. He watched me carefully as I undressed.

I put my foot in and jerked it back because it was really hot. "Tyler, that's too hot."

"That's how I like it."

I sat down on the side and put my feet in until I could get used to the temperature. Slowly I worked my way in a little at a time.

Tyler was enjoying watching me squirm. Finally he said, "Just get in quick. It's easier."

So I jumped in, and for a minute, it was hard to breath. I knew now why Tyler had invited me over. It wasn't because he wanted a friend to play games with or to hang out with. He wanted to do things that were secret, things that had to always stay a secret. He knew I wouldn't tell. I knew where he was coming from. I didn't want anyone else to know this side of my life either. He reached over and kissed me.

"What about Anna?"

"She knows not to come in here." He kissed me again.

"Tyler."

"What?"

"Trust me; you don't want to try this in a Jacuzzi."

"Why?"

"Trust me, I know."

"Where do you suggest then?"

"The steam room" We both got out and went in the steam room.

When it was over, Tyler opened the door and had that same shit-eating grin on his face as before. It was getting dark, and I knew I had to go home. We walked back to the laundry room and found that Anna had folded my clothes and set them on the dryer. I put them back on and could hear the rain hitting the roof. I lived kind of far away, and on the way back, there was more downhill than uphill. But I wasn't looking forward to getting cold and soaking wet twice in a day.

Tyler handed me an envelope, and I knew there was money in it.

I handed it back to him and told him, "I came here because I wanted to." I hesitated and hoped he would offer me a ride home. But he didn't get the hint, so I told him good-bye and left. I was soaked before I got to the gate at the end of the driveway.

It was late, and I was freezing by the time I got home. It was too late to walk through the front door, so I went in through the side garage door. It was quiet, and I snuck into my bedroom without my parents hearing me.

Thursday after school I walked to the shopping center. Roger was waiting for me just like Brian had said he would be.

Roger said, "Hey, Timmy, get in."

I opened the passenger door and jumped in. "So, Timmy, how was your day?"

"Great! How was yours?"

I couldn't believe we were having a friendly conversation. In the pass it seemed Roger tolerated me at best, for Brian's sake.

"We got a lot done this week." I didn't know who he meant by *whether* he meant people at work or people in the group.

"Where are we going?"

"Rick and Todd's house"

"Will Brian be there?"

"Maybe" I know Troy will be there."

Shit, I knew I was in trouble. I knew they were going to start another movie, and there was nothing I could do about it. "What did you guys get done this week?" I asked, fishing for more information so I could be prepared.

"We worked on Rick and Todd's studio."

I was quiet for a few minutes, deep in thought about what this day had in store for me.

Roger broke the silence. "Timmy, you're not just Brian's boy anymore" your community property."

I hesitated a minute and then asked, "What is community property?"

"The whole group owns you."

"What?"

"That's right, the group."

Making sure I understood him completely, I asked, "Who is the group?"

"Bill Rick Todd, or even Brian, That includes me."

This whole conversation was useless, they all did what they wanted, and nothing else mattered.

"The only difference now is that Brian knows about the movies, and he won't be there to protect you anymore."

After hearing that last comment I had to ask. "Do you want to hurt me, Roger?"

"No."

"Do the other guys want to hurt me?"

"No."

"Roger, if they do try to hurt me, will you protect me? You guys already know I can act. I don't need to feel real pain to act like it hurts." I had to get him to understand what it felt like to be me. I already went along with the script, and I could act out all the emotions they needed without them having to scare me and hurt me. He could tell I was nervous because my voice started shaking a little.

I guess I reached some part of his soul with that plea and he answered, "Timmy, no one wants to hurt you, and I wouldn't let them if they did."

I knew it was a false promise, but it felt good to think I may have one person on my side for the events ahead.

I looked out the window as Roger drove, and a thousand thoughts went through my head. Did Brian still love me? I had lied to him and, in a way, cheated on him. I had embarrassed him in front of other guys in the group, who knew about the movie before him. I wasn't in control of my decisions because they had me at every turn. I could be blackmailed from any angle, but I still felt like I had let Brian down somehow. My parents couldn't help me out;

they would never understand. How did this madness get so far out of hand. My mom would beat me and have dad's blessing while she did it. I would be too embarrassed for them to know any part of the last couple years. I was stuck, and I knew it—nothing new there. I needed to do what had worked in the past—just put it out of my mind and act like it was all normal. But my mind was spinning, and I almost started to cry. I knew this would totally piss Roger off, so I coughed a little to clear my throat and put it all so far back in my mind that I wouldn't think anymore.

FANTASIES

We pulled into Rick and Todd's driveway and got out of the car. Rick met me at the door and gave me a big hug, lifting me off the ground. "I've missed you," he said.

Before I knew it, Todd came up and did the same thing, although not as enthusiastically. But he gave me a hug just the same.

I told them I missed them too because that was the polite thing to say. I wished I had the guts to tell them how they had hurt me in unimaginable ways and walk out the door. But that was just a fantasy I carried around to help keep me sane.

I saw Troy across the room and knew he really *was* glad to see me—at least he was glad for the right reasons. We had become pretty close, and I did my best to watch out for him.

The guys started talking, and Troy asked me, "Have you seen the garage lately?"

"No. I've been gone remember?"

He opened the door. They had dry walled the three walls so that it didn't look like a garage anymore. They were making improvements all the time. The ceiling was still open so they could hang us from the rafters when needed. Mirrors covered the walls. Basically all the same sick stuff was there, but Rick and Todd had altered the dark and gloomy look, brightening it up so they could catch much better details when filming. I felt sick to my stomach. I had felt exposed before. Now it would be even more intense.

Troy could see the horror on my face. "Are you all right?" he asked.

"No. I don't want to be here." I was trying to catch my breath.

Troy grabbed my arm and pulled me out of the room. I leaned against the wall and slid down until I was sitting on the floor. I put my head between my legs and cried uncontrollably. Troy sat down next to me and put his arm around me to console me.

"What's wrong, Timmy? What's wrong?" he kept asking.

I couldn't even speak. All the emotion of the pain and humiliation I had experienced was suffocating me—shutting my brain off and stopping me from breathing right.

The men heard the sound and came to check it out. "What the hell is going on?" Roger asked.

Troy tried to answer but realized he didn't even know what to say.

Todd yelled, "Stop that crying and act your age! I'm sick of it!"

Rick found that statement ironic and told him, "He is acting his age, you idiot!"

Then he bent down and stood me on my feet, put his arm around me, and walked me to his office. He sat me down next to him on the couch and said, "Okay Timmy, relax and tell me what's wrong."

I still couldn't speak. I knew what I wanted to say would only piss him off, so I stayed silent.

A few minutes later, Carlos walked in, and I was so thankful. Rick stood up, and Carlos asked, "What's wrong?"

Rick said, "I don't know. Maybe he will talk to you."

"Timmy, are you all right?" Carlos asked. I nodded my head yes, hoping Rick would just leave the room so I could talk alone to Carlos. Instead he walked behind his desk and sat down.

Carlos sat next to me and asked, "So what's going on? Troy said you just freaked out. Why?"

"I got scared."

"Why?"

"I don't know," I mumbled.

Carlos put his arm around me, and I started to cry again. Finally, I could talk again and said, "Brian told me I was done. I thought I would never be here again. Brian told me I would be free, but I'm not. It's even worse than before."

Rick asked, "How's that?"

"Roger told me I was community property I'm no longer Brian's but I belong to the whole group."

"I hate to break it to you, kid, but you always were community property. You always belonged to the group. That's what Brian didn't understand."

That didn't make me feel any better.

Carlos asked Rick, "Can I have a moment alone with him?"

Rick stood up to leave. He came over to me first. He grabbed my chin and made me look him in the eye. "Didn't I tell you I wouldn't let anything bad happen to you?"

I just nodded my head.

"Well nothing has changed. If any of the men mistreat you, you tell me. We have new rules to make sure no one gets hurt. If they get out of line, you tell me. If what you say is true, then they have to leave. Do you understand me?"

I nodded my head yes again.

"And today, you will know what we are going to do before we do it." Then he left the room.

I looked at Carlos and said, "I can't believe you're here."

"I told you I would be. Are you okay?"

"It freaked me out when I walked into the garage."

"Why?"

"You saw the movies; you know the stuff that goes on in there."

"I saw two of the movies, and they were great. How many are there?"

He could see the shock on my face. It was embarrassing to me that Carlos watch any of them"

"How many movies did you make?"

I just looked at him, defeated. I wanted him to understand that I was made to make the movies. But Carlos was like Nick, and the whole thing excited him.

"I don't know how many movies there are. Or what happens to them when they are done? Who gets to see them? What if someone I know sees them?"

"That won't happen."

"You don't know that."

"Yes, I do."

"How" I thought no one was supposed to watch the ones they watched either! I thought they were only for Rick and Todd. I never dreamed you or Brian or, worse yet, some kid named Tyler would see them. But you all did. As a matter of fact, I'm afraid the videos might have left the group."

"You worry too much, Timmy. Just relax."

"You're going to be in the next one, Carlos. What if someone in your family sees it? Or someone at school?"

He thought for a minute and just laughed. "Come on. Nothing like that is going to happen." He stood up and reached for my hands and pulled me up. "Come on, cheer up! At least I'm here instead of Nick." I tried to put on a fake smile. "Are you telling me you would rather have Nick than me?"

I finally smiled and told him, "I would take you over Nick any day."

We walked into the kitchen where everyone was waiting. Todd asked, "Is he all right?"

Carlos put his arm around me and says, "Yeah, he's fine."

They told us to sit down. I had Troy and Carlos on each side of me. They told us what was going to happen in the first scene. There would be no adults in this movie, just kids. They would be standing on the sidelines telling us what to do.

We walked into the new and improved House of Pain and got ready to start filming. Carlos puts on a Zorro mask, it did nothing to hide his identity, and actually, he looked cool. Troy and I put on the wrist restraints that hooked up to a bar that was controlled by chains hanging from the rafters. The higher they lifted us, the closer our bodies got to each other. Finally our bodies were completely touching each other. We gently pushed away only to swing right back to each other. This was enough stimulation for two young boys who got excited easily.

The men were talking, and we could tell they liked it so far. Carlos walked around us with a black cloth whip. It looked like a leather belt that would hurt, but it didn't. He could swing it really hard, and it didn't bother us at all. Troy's head was on my shoulder, and we were acting like we were in pain.

Then Troy whispered to me, "You're poking me." We both started to laugh.

"What the hell are you two laughing about?" Carlos sounds pissed "He keeps poking me," Troy said.

"Well, he keeps poking me," I said.

Then all three of us laughed. The guys stopped filming, and Todd got mad, while Rick and Roger were laughing. They lowered the rod to give our arms time to rest and put blood back onto our hands, but mostly because they couldn't get us to stop laughing. We had a break for about fifteen minutes.

When that was over, Todd pulled out a real whip and threatened us, "If you laugh again, we'll use the real one."

I looked at Troy and he looked at me, and we both knew he wasn't kidding.

We all went back to playing our parts. With the new lighting, the room was getting really hot. We were sweating and tired after a few hours of filming, and the guys finally called it quits. Rick let us boys go into the Jacuzzi. We used to have to swim to the Jacuzzi because it was in the middle of the pool, but they had built a bridge so you could walk to it. I still preferred to jump in the pool and swim over. The water was heated, and it felt great. By the time I swam over the boys were sitting up to their necks in the hot water. I always had trouble getting in because the water felt too hot. I had to inch my way in. Carlos always enjoyed watching me squirm.

Carlos was talking excitedly to Troy about his part in the movie. He was a lot like Nick in that respect. Troy and I, on the other hand, were scared to death wondering who would watch it.

Troy went under the water and grabbed my feet, forcing me under. "There, Timmy, you don't have to struggle anymore. You're in." I smiled even though I didn't think it was funny.

We played around until the men joined us.

The guys were talking about the group party coming up on Saturday. I had almost forgotten about it. It had been about two months since I'd been to one. That seemed like a lifetime ago. The thought of being exposed and at the group mercy made me shiver. I could see that Troy was nervous too, so I consoled him. "Don't worry, Troy. I'll be there to protect you."

He smiled.

I got out of the Jacuzzi and dove into the pool. The water seemed cold now, but I knew my body would adjust.

Troy jumped in after me and yelled, "It's too cold."

"No. It's just right."

I swam under him and pulled him down. He gagged, and I laughed "Now we're even."

"Let's go back in the Jacuzzi," Troy said.

"I don't want to hear them talk about the party."

"Are you afraid that you're going to get it?"

"No. Bill told me I wouldn't be punished."

"Why?"

"Because it wasn't my fault"

"I still think you're going to get it."

"Thanks, Troy. I feel better now."

"Sorry, I just think you are."

I swam away so I wouldn't have to hear it anymore.

Troy followed. "How did it feel to be out of the group?" He asked the question because, after you had been in for a while, you were made to think that there wasn't a life worth living outside the group. That's what Carlos and Nick had been taught" Hell it what I believed. If you were in the group, you were special—above regular kids; you were a chosen one of the select few. You were given love, money, and attention. I guess we had all been looking for parts of that when we were recruited.

"It was scary at first. I felt lonely, but it got better as time went by."

"Hey, what are you guys talking about?" Rick asked.

"Nothing," Troy answered.

"Then get back in here before your balls shrivel up," Rick demanded"

Troy jumped in quickly, and while I was making my way in, Rick joked, "Too late for you, Timmy."

I got in quicker so they would quit looking.

Roger said, "Carlos, get your stuff so we can go. You too, Troy, I'm taking you both home tonight."

I thought Roger was my ride too, so I asked, "What about me?"

"Rick will take you home later."

I didn't act disappointed or upset even though I was. If I showed it that would really pissed Todd off, and I knew I wasn't in a passion to make him mad now, It would be twice as hard on me later. Carlos and Troy got out and they both gave me a look that said better you than me.

Rick and Todd stayed in the Jacuzzi another ten to fifteen minutes giving Roger time to leave. So Then they both stared at me. Todd said, "Wow Rick. Timmy handled that pretty well."

"We sure missed you while you were gone," Rick added. "We didn't think Brian would ever give up your location."

"So . . . you thought you could get away from us?" Todd's voice got loud.

I felt like I was at an inquisition. I had no idea what they had in store for me, and I didn't want to piss them off.

"Todd, why are you getting mad at me" You know I always do what I'm told."

"Then why did you leave?" Todd asked.

"I was doing what Brian told me to do."

"Well, now you are going to do what we want you to do!" Todd demanded.

He was looking for a fight where there was none. I just wanted to get it over with. They led me to the new studio, where all their sick, twisted toys were. They tied me down to that beam that they'd made famous in their films. They put the ball in my mouth so they couldn't hear me scream. They did unspeakable things to me, the worst ever. Not only did they intentionally cause terrible pain, but they took me to a new level of humiliation. They used objects and said and did things that I didn't know humans were capable of.

When they were done, they knew it had gone too far. I could see it in their eyes,they were both ashamed. As soon as they took the straps off, I yanked the ball out of my mouth. I was crying and gasping for air. I couldn't talk. My mind couldn't take in what had just happened, and I was going into shock. I stood there staring at both of them with shock and horror on my face as blood dripped down my legs from my butt. Even after all I had been through, I had never had these kinds of injuries before. I could barely stand, but I used all my strength to walk out of that room.

They walked me to a bathroom to clean me up. I knew the things they had done were not allowed, and someone was going to pay! Rick was begging me to forgive him, telling me he was sorry. Todd walked out, mad because Rick was apologizing. Rick cleaned me up, and I got dressed. I had stopped crying, but I was still in shock from the trauma of it all.

Rick walked me to the living room, and he was still trying to get me to talk and accept his apology.

"Knock it off, Rick!" Todd yelled. "If you keep apologizing to him, he'll believe we actually did something wrong."

I couldn't keep silent anymore. Even though my body was still shaking, I yelled, "I'm telling Bill!"

That must have been the magic word because it stopped Todd in his tracks. They both looked at each other, and I saw fear in their eyes.

"He told me that no one was allowed to hurt me. He would protect me and I was to tell him if anyone got out of line with me."

Todd bowed his head, and Rick said, "Look, we're sorry."

Todd pulled out his wallet and said, "Come on, Timmy, we can come to some kind of an agreement, can't we?"

I didn't know what to say. It had taken everything I had to say what I already said. I sat down on the couch and something inside me told me not to push Todd too far. I kind of felt like my life could be in danger at this point. Just thinking like that gave me goose bumps. He handed me five hundred dollars, and I took it. Then I looked at Rick, and he pulled some more money out of his pocket. They were rich, and I knew the money meant nothing to them, but staying in the group meant everything. And they had put that in jeopardy when they'd crossed over the line tonight.

Todd asked, "Is it a deal?"

I nodded my head yes.

Rick drove me home, and we were both silent. The silence was so great it sounded loud to me. The radio was off and, with our windows rolled up, the other cars just made a muffled sound. I knew it was so late I would probably get in trouble at home, but that was the least of my worries tonight.

When we got close to my house, Rick broke the silence, "Timmy, you can't tell anyone. I know you are good at keeping secrets. Can you keep this one?"

I nodded my head yes and pointed to my house, and Rick drove past it a little before letting me out.

"You don't live that far."

I just gave him a look that said, drop dead.

"What's wrong?"

"I can't walk into the house this late without getting an ass whooping. I can't have all this money on me. You are going to have to hold it for me. I will keep forty, and you keep the rest."

"How bad do you think you will get it?"

"I'm thinking after what you did to me, an ass whooping is nothing." But I knew that wasn't really true. My mom could be ruthless when she was mad. I shrugged my shoulders and walked away as best I could.

SECRETS

Just as I feared, Mom was waiting behind the door holding a belt. I opened the door slowly and looked inside. She grabbed my hair and pulled me the rest of the way in. She pushed me to the floor, and the beating began with a fury. Mom was wild when she was angry, with an uncontrollable rage. All I could do was try to crawl away from her. In the meantime, she was swinging with all her might, and I was praying she wouldn't last long. I headed to my room, covering my head as best I could and crying and screaming. She did get tired of the belt, but she was too mad to stop the beating. She punched and kicked me until she had no more strength left.

After that, I made it to my room, where she looked at me and slams the door shut. I was crying hard. I hurt inside and out. I crawled under my bed and rolled up into a ball and cried myself to sleep.

The next morning, I was so sore I could barely move. It wasn't so much what Mom had done but what Rick and Todd had done. I felt like I had been torn apart.

Tommy walked in and yelled, "Timmy!"

That made me jump. With all the excitement last night, I hadn't set my alarm clock for school. I hurt so bad I knew I wasn't going anyways.

"Tommy, I'm sick."

"What, from the beating you got last night?"

I shrugged my shoulders for an answer.

He left the room and informed Mom of my illness. She was already up and dressed and ready to leave the house.

She threw the door open so hard it hit the wall and said, "You're not screwing up my day. I have plans to go shopping with your

10

grandma and Aunt Stacy." She touched my forehead, and it felt hot to her. "You're running a temperature. Will you be okay to stay home alone?"

I nodded, thanking God that she had plans today. She kissed me on the forehead and left my room.

Tommy said, "You faker."

Then he opened up his backpack and took out a big box of candy.

"What's that for?"

"I'm selling them at school and making double the profit." Then he showed me the cash he had.

"Wow! That's a great idea!"

Tommy was really feeling good about himself when he left my room. This gave me a great way to justify my money if I ever got caught with some of it.

My body was aching horribly, and I rolled over and went back to sleep. I woke up around noon, and I could barely walk to the kitchen to get something to eat. I fixed a nice hot bath and sat back and enjoyed having the house to myself for a little while. The bath made me feel better. Since there was nothing else I could do, I went back to bed and slept until school was out.

When Tommy came home, he slammed the front door and woke me up. He opened my bedroom door and asked, "You're still in bed?" He pulled out a wad of bills and said, "See, I sold them all."

"Wow! How much money did you make?"

"Around twenty-five dollars"

"That's great!"

I was happy for him, even though he had no idea of the money I had. At least his didn't have all the strings attached that mine did.

I fell back to sleep and woke when it was dark to Tommy saying, "Timmy, phone!" He opened my door. "It's Tyler."

I rolled out of bed slowly and made my way to the kitchen.

Tommy watched me walk. "What the hell is wrong with you?" he asked.

"I don't feel good."

"Fine Just quit walking like you have a corn cob stuck up your butt."

I just gave him a look and turned away. He had no idea, and there was no way I could even begin to explain. I picked up the phone. "Hey, Tyler, what's going on?"

"Can you spend the night tonight and tomorrow and help me get ready for my party?"

"Sorry, Tyler, I'm sick and have been in bed all day."

"You'll feel better by tomorrow, wont' you?" I could hear in his tone that he was afraid I would disappoint him.

"Yeah, I'm sure I'll be better by tomorrow."

"Good. Can you come in the morning and help me get ready?"

"What time?"

"Around 10:00."

"How will I get to your house? You're not going to make me ride my bike over there, are you?"

He laughed. "No. Maybe Anna will come get you."

"Well okay, find out and call me back." I hadn't even asked my mom yet if I could go.

Tyler called back. "Anna can pick you up at 9:00."

I gave him directions to my house and hung up. I really didn't want to go to his party, but I didn't want to let Tyler down. That would piss Bill off and he was starting to be nice to me, and I didn't want to get on his bad side. I knew what that was like. It wasn't pretty.

My dad came home, and it was nice to have him without Mom. He asked us boys if we were hungry and went to the kitchen and started cooking dinner. Tommy and I were both surprised, so we went into the kitchen just to watch this cosmic event.

He was in a good mood and started frying hamburger to make tacos. He asked Tommy about his new business and listened. When they were done talking, I asked him if I could go to Tyler's party tomorrow. He smiled which was a good sign, and then to my surprise said, "No." I was shocked, but I knew not to ask why.

"Dad, can I call him to tell him I can't come?"

"Yes."

Tyler answered the phone, and I said, "I asked my dad if I could go to your party, and he said no. I'm really sorry." I knew he was really disappointed, and he hung up the phone quickly.

I went back to watching Dad cook and talk to Tommy. I was relieved that I had gotten out of going to the party. I was in no shape for any social events right now. With Tyler, I felt like he didn't just want me for a friend; he wanted much more from me. A few minutes later, the phone rang, and I answered because I was closest.

"Timmy, it's me, Bill." I knew who it was right away, and I was scared. "Is your dad there?"

"Yes."

"Put him on."

I nervously told my dad, "It's for you."

Dad picked it up and started talking. I walked around the corner to listen. I could only hear Dad's side of the conversation. He wasn't getting mad, like I thought he would. It wasn't long before Dad was telling Bill what he did for a living. He even laughed a few times. They talked around fifteen minutes or so, and Dad hung up and finished cooking.

Tommy and Dad went back to talking. Tommy yelled that dinner was ready. It was fun, just us three guys sitting at the table, no yelling or shoving food or getting slapped for not eating food you hated.

Dad asked, "Timmy, how do you know Tyler?"

I'd known this was coming, but it still made me nervous. I didn't know what to say. I didn't know what Bill and Dad had talked about. I just sat there and didn't answer.

"I don't think my question is too hard,"

"Excuse, Me, Dad, I'm sorry. I know him from a friend at school."

"How old is he?"

I nervously answered, "Just a little older than me."

He would be suspicious if I told him the truth.

"Well, I talked to his dad, and I guess you can go tomorrow. Are they rich?"

"Very!"

"How rich" Tommy asked.

"Put it this way, his house is bigger than our block. They have a playroom with a bowling alley in it."

"Wow! Can I go?" Tommy asked.

Dad cut in, "You be nice to Tyler. He really wants you at his party. Plus, his dad has a side job for me that will pay a lot, and we really need the money." Then dad smiled. He had no idea what it took to make that family happy.

The next morning, Anna picked me up. I jumped in the passenger seat, and we took off.

"Timmy, you live in a nice neighborhood."

"Thanks."

"If I ask you a question, Timmy, will you keep it a secret?"

"I'm the Fort Knox of secrets."

"Good. Because I would get fired if you told."

I wanted to say, *Then don't ask*, but I didn't.

"Why are you here?"

"What do you mean?"

"Why are you hanging around Tyler? Why do you call his dad Bill?"

Oh, shit! It's not his name I thought. I just shrugged my shoulders like I didn't know.

"I know what they are doing to you, Timmy." And it makes me sick"

"How do you know?"

"I'm not blind. I've worked for 'Bill,' as I am supposed to call him also when you are around, for three years. I know he's into boys. Why do you come over? Is it the money?"

"No! You have no idea." I answered nervously. I couldn't even explain it to myself. How could I begin to tell her.

"Then what"

"I don't want to talk about this anymore." I just sat there quietly.

"Are you going to tell on me?" she asked.

"No."

"Thanks. I really need my job."

"I have a boy your age, Timmy. It's a great house, and Bill pays really well. But I would never let my son go over there. Why do your parents let you go?"

I looked out the window and said softly, "They don't know." I looked back at her, pleading in my expression for her to keep my secret also.

We pulled up to the gate, and she entered the code. As she was doing, this she explained, "The number for the gate is 1225; just remembers Christmas. Use the back door because it's always unlocked. I'll see you later."

"Aren't you coming in?"

"No. I got the day off. Hey, Timmy, you will keep our secret, won't you?"

"I will if you will." I smiled to let her know it meant a lot that she cared, but it couldn't change anything in my life right now. And Anna would be out of a job,

I walked through the back door, past the laundry room, and into the kitchen, calling out, "Hey, it's me, Timmy."

When I received no answer, I kept going into the living room, calling out again.

This time I got an answer from Bill, "I'm in here." He was in his office doing some reading.

"Sir, it's me."

"I know who you are, Timmy. Come in." I walked to the front of his desk. "Glad you could make it. Come a little closer." I walked around his desk, which looked bigger than my whole bedroom and stood in front of him. He reached out and touched my arm. "How did you get that?" he asked.

"I was out too late, and Mom caught me."

"Why were you out late?"

I was wondering why he even cared. "Rick and Todd had me out late."

"Why?"

I just shrugged my shoulders as if I didn't know. He started unbuttoning my shirt, and I thought it was for his pleasure, but it wasn't. "What about these bruises? Did your mom give you these?"

It was easier to answer him with my back to him. "Yes."

He turned me around. "Are you sure?" His voice was sounding angrier.

I felt like he could see right through me. Plus, he was so damn intimidating.

My voice quivered, but I answered, "I'm sure."

"Timmy, you can come to me with anything. You know that, don't you?"

I nodded yes. I believed him, but I had heard this before, and it never made any difference.

"I mean anything—money, family, friends, or even the guys in the group. Timmy, I want to look out for you."

I smiled at him. I loved the sound of someone watching over me. It was hard not to hope that things may improve.

"Will you let me?"

I looked him in the eye this time and said, "Yes."

"Good. How did you get these bruises then? Was it Rick and Todd?"

"It really was my mom."

He seemed surprised by my answer, but it was the truth. My mom had put these bruises on me, but it wasn't nearly as bad as it could have been. Rick and Todd had done damage on the inside that no one could see, not even Bill.

"Timmy, Tyler is still asleep. Why don't you go wake him up?"

I turned to run out of the room, and Bill said, "Timmy, do me a favor and don't talk to Tyler anymore about the movies you've been in. He wants to be in one, and that isn't going to happen."

"No problem."

I ran down the hall and up the stairs to Tyler's room. I opened his door slowly and let my eyes get used to the dark. I ran to his bed and jumped right on top of him. It scared him at first until he figured out it was me.

"You little shit!" Tyler said, and this made me laugh.

16

He jumped up and landed on me. I moaned in pain.

"Tyler, stop! You win!"

It was his turn to laugh now. He lay back down, and we both caught our breath.

He looked at me and asked, "Where is your shirt?"

"Downstairs."

"Are you okay? Why is it downstairs?"

I just shrugged my shoulders for an answer.

"Does my dad have it?"

"Yeah"

He looked disappointed, and I realized that he was jealous.

"What did my dad do to you?"

I laughed, "Nothing actually. He saw the bruises that my mom had given me."

"Really," Tyler replied and turned on the light.

"Look." I showed them to Tyler.

"So is that all that happened"

"Yes. That's all. I promise."

That made him happy once again. But I was thinking that Tyler was weird. He couldn't be that naïve. He had to know what the hell was going on around here. Hell, he'd seen the movies, and that's how he'd come to pick me. His dad was the one who'd set up everything for me to get to know Tyler. His dad was the one who'd made sure I was here today.

"Timmy, take a shower with me."

"No. Your dad said no funny stuff or he'll kick my ass."

"He meant at the party tonight."

I knew what Bill had meant, but I was acting stupid to get out of it.

"Come on, Timmy. That's not what he meant."

I didn't want to. I was still sore from Rick and Todd's torture session.

"Please, Tyler; I don't want to right now."

All the while, he was dragging me off the bed and into the bathroom. He blocked the door and started to undress. I wondered what had happened to that shy kid I'd met a few weeks ago. You could tell he was a lot like his dad and was used to getting his way. I pictured myself disobeying him and snap kicking him in the nuts, but I knew his dad would kill me. I knew my dad wanted side work from Bill. I knew all the reasons it was wrong and all the reasons why I was taking off my clothes for Tyler.

In the shower, Tyler said to me, "Don't be mad."

"I'm not."

"What's wrong then?"

"It's just that last time . . ."

"Last time what?" he asked with a much deeper concern than I would expect from him.

"Last time, you screwed me then sent me home. You got what you wanted, and then you were done. I had to ride my bike home in the dark, and it was raining and really cold. I live pretty far away, and none of that mattered to you. I thought we were friends I cried"

"I'm sorry, Timmy. I wasn't thinking. And we are friends."

"I feel like I'm here for one reason, and when you're done with me, you'll be mean to me."

"Shit, Timmy, I've never been mean to you. And the other night I just wasn't thinking. I'm sorry. Are we okay?"

"Yeah" I answered, not knowing why I'd opened up like that. I really didn't care. I was used to people using me. But venting like that helped me gain a little control in this whole situation.

"Are we okay?" Tyler asked one more time to make sure.

"Yeah, we're okay."

We finished with the shower and other stuff. The whole time, I was wondering how I had gotten to this point in my life. I was a few month from turning eleven years old. I was used to be the innocent victim being used by others; now I was becoming one of the players. I felt like that gave me power over them at times, even though I knew the truth about who held all the real power—the adults. But I was learning how to manipulate the guys so I didn't walk away empty-handed. They needed to pay well for what they were getting.

Deep down, I knew I wanted out of this life. I wanted out of the abuse from my mom and the lack of concern from my dad. I wanted out from the group of men who demanded my body and soul, or at least it seemed that way. I wished myself away to a tropical island where I lived alone; no one would have any expectations of me. I prayed to God to help change my life. At times, I even thought about killing myself. But I chickened out because Mom said people went to hell for that. And the way she explained hell put chills up and down my spine. I felt like I deserved hell for the choices I was now making on my own. But after some of the most horrifying experiences I had gone through, just maybe I had visited it a few times already. I knew I surely did not want to live there forever.

We sat on the bed, and I cautiously tried to ask Tyler something I'd been wondering about. "Does your dad . . . ?" There was a long pause.

"Does my dad what?"

"You know, does he do things to you?"

"No! That's gross; you're sick. Why, does your dad?"

"No!"

"Why does your mom beat you?"

"She's a bitch. What can I say" I paused.

"What about your mom?"

"She died when I was born."

"I'm sorry."

"Why does your dad let her beat you?"

"I don't really know. Maybe he's doesn't know everything that goes on."

"Tell him. I'm sure he would make it stop."

I just shrugged my shoulders and looked for a way out of this conversation.

"So, Tyler, why are you having a party tonight?"

"Oh shit! What time is it?" He jumped out of bed and finished getting dressed.

I followed his lead and did the same thing. We ran down the stairs, and Tyler was calling for his dad. Bill was still in his office and Tyler hurried in there. I waited on the bottom of the stairs, not sure if too much of Bill was a good thing yet. Tyler yelled for me to join him, so I did.

Bill said, "Tyler, go show them where the tables are to be set up." Then he turned to me and said, "Timmy, stay here. I need to talk to you."

Tyler left the office and called back to me. "Come find me when you're done."

"Sit down," Bill said.

I sat down in a huge chair across from him, and this made me feel even smaller.

He smiled at me and asked, "Why are you here, Timmy?"

"Sir" I didn't understand this line of questioning. They were the ones who'd invited me.

"Are you here because of me or Tyler?"

"Both, I guess."

"Do you like Tyler?"

"Yes, sir"

Then he opened up his desk drawer and handed me an envelope.

I knew it had money in it. "You don't have to pay me."

"Why not Timmy" Do you think you are like us? Like Tyler?"

"No, sir"

"Damn straight you're not! You're hired help."

I just sat there and kept a straight face, even though I felt like crying. He looked really mad and I was so young I wasn't quite sure what he meant by that.

"Keep the money, Timmy."

I stood up and put the money in my back pocket.

"Do you understand what I am saying?"

I nodded yes, but really I felt kind of lost. He made me so nervous half of the time that I couldn't think straight. He was the kind of guy who was pure power and extremely intimidating. And I'd never forgotten what he did to me the last time when I made him mad. I'd do anything not to go there again.

Bill was still talking while my mind was spinning, and finally he snapped his fingers at me. "Timmy, are you hearing anything I am saying?"

I didn't know what I had missed, so to be safe, I shrugged my shoulders.

"No! What's wrong with you "he snapped.

I just shrugged my shoulders again. "You listen here! You answer me with words, young man!"

My voice was quivering, but I hoped I was talking loud enough for him to hear me, "You get mad at me. It scares me."

"Didn't I tell you I wouldn't hurt you?"

"Yes."

"Well then get a hold of yourself and go help Tyler. I swear, Timmy; I can't even talk to you without you freaking out."

I stood up and walked to the door and turned around, "I'm sorry."

"Me too" Just go help Tyler please."

I stopped by the bathroom and took a minute to get back to normal before heading to the backyard where Tyler was. The catering company was already there setting up. I helped set up tables and lights and put up decorations. This took a couple of hours. When we were done, we stepped back and looked at our work and felt proud. It kind of reminded me of some of the parties I had been to with the group and it gave me chills just thinking about it.

It was only 2:00 p.m., and we had four hours before the party was to start. Tyler asked, "What do you want to do now?"

"What can we do?"

"Do you want to go to the mall?"

"Do we have time?"

"Yeah, wait here for a minute."

Tyler returned with his dad, and we got into the car and left for the mall. Bill told us we had two hours and he would be back to pick us up. He gave Tyler some money and reminded me that I had the envelope from this morning.

We got out of the car and Tyler asked, "What envelope?"

I almost forgot and pulled it out of my back pocket.

"What's in it?"

"Money"

"How much money"

"I don't know."

"Open it."

I wasn't fast enough, so he grabbed it from me and tore it open. "Three hundred dollars" Tyler was mad, "Is he paying you to be with me?"

"Tyler, I tried to give it back to him, but your dad got mad at me and made me take it."

Tyler wasn't hearing anything I said. I was still trying to explain and he yelled, "You piece of shit!" and threw the envelope at me, the money falling to the ground.

He ran into the mall, and I picked up the money. I ran after him but couldn't find him anywhere. I spent the whole two hours looking for him, not spending any of the money that had caused this whole problem.

I was out front on time for Bill to pick me up. Tyler was already in the car, so I got in the backseat. I was scared, mad, and confused and on top of all that, my feelings were hurt. After I shut the door, I couldn't help but start to cry.

Tyler turned around to look at me, and I begged, "Please, just take me home."

Bill put the car in park and said, "Not another word!"

Tyler said, "Timmy, I'm sorry."

Bill demanded, "Why are you saying sorry?"

I pulled the money out of my pocket and threw it in the front seat and said, "I told you I didn't want your money. You're right, Bill; I'm not like you guys. Please just take me home."

Bill turned around and looked me in the eye and said, "Not another word! Do you understand?"

I nodded while Bill put the car in gear and headed home. By now I figured I had truly blown it and had said too much. I was getting really scared. Bill pulled into the garage and came around the car and jerked me out of the backseat.

He marched me through the house. Tyler was begging for my sake, "Dad, don't hurt him. You know it's not his fault."

Bill turned to him. "You shut your mouth!"

Tyler bowed his head quickly to show his obedience.

Bill led me down the hall and past his office, past the game room and a couple more doors. With each step, my anxiety rose. I'd seen him in this kind of mood before; there was no good end to this story. He stopped at a door and pulled out a set of keys and unlocked the door.

I couldn't believe my eyes. Bill had a room similar to Rick and Todd's House of Pain. I wondered who had copied whom. I wondered how many of the guys had these rooms at their home.

Bill grabbed the back of my neck and led me to a rack. It was the same one Rick and Todd used when they had beaten the hell out of me. I could barely speak I was so shocked, but I knew I had to try. "You said you wouldn't hurt me again like that."

"Did I?"

"What did I do wrong? Bill, please." I begged for my life.

"Sometimes people have to be put in their place." He grabbed my shirt and pulled it off as I fought to keep it on. He slapped me and threatens, "I swear to God, Timmy, if you fight me, you'll get it twice as bad."

I already knew what a ruthless bastard he could be, and he proved it once again. He put the straps on my wrists on the first beam and lifted up my legs so that my stomach rested on the second beam. Then he pulled off my pants and underwear and strapped down my ankles on the third beam. The rack was set up so your butt was a little higher than your back and head. This exposed everything and left you completely defenseless.

Then to my surprise, he left the room. I was crying, of course—not yet hysterical but getting close.

I could have died of embarrassment when he returned with Tyler. I could tell by the surprised look on Tyler's face that he had never seen this room before. Tyler begged, "Dad, please, it's not his fault."

"Then it must be your fault," his dad replied.

"Yes," Tyler answered.

"Then you take off your clothes, and I'll put you on the rack."

"No, Dad!"

"Then pick up that whip."

Tyler pulled back from his dad.

"Boy, you pick up that whip, or it will be done to you!"

Tyler picked up the whip. I was in shock. I couldn't believe this was happening.

Bill looked at me, "Timmy, I'll give you a choice. Do you want a beating from Tyler or me?"

Hell that was a no-brainer. "Tyler," I answered. I was surprised I even got the word out.

Tyler barely swung the whip, and this enraged Bill. He grabbed the whip and lays a hard one on my butt. I flinched and yelled in pain. Then he told Tyler, "I'll tell you what, he gets ten from you, but for every one I don't think is hard enough, I give him one. So he gets ten from you or twenty from both of us."

Tyler took the whip again and hit me a little harder. I jumped. Bill grabbed the whip and hits me twice as hard. I screamed in pain and begged him to stop. Then Tyler took the whip one more time and gave me nine really hard ones on my back and butt, really fast. I was squirming and screaming.

"Now that wasn't so bad, was it?" Bill said Tyler.

It sounded like Tyler was crying too. "No, sir"

"You take care of him," Bill said. Then he grabbed my hair and threatened me, "I swear to God, Timmy, you'd better not ever disrespect me again." Then to Tyler, he said, "You'd better hurry up. People are going to start arriving in about an hour." He slammed the door behind him to finish making his point.

Tyler undid all the straps and I moaned as he helped me off the beams. I tried to stand but fell because my legs were asleep. He helped me to my feet, all the while telling me how sorry he was, begging me not to hate him. He walked me past Bill's office, through the living room, and to the staircase that led to his bedroom. He never grabbed my clothes, so I was completely naked. I was completely defeated by now. He could have led me anywhere. I was totally submissive. I felt like I was nothing.

He went into the bathroom and got the shower temperature ready for me. I stepped in, flinching when the water hit the whip marks on my body. I tried not to moan, but the sound still escaped my mouth. I just stood there looking down at the drain as the water rolled off my body. My mind was spinning in circles. I had thought I was done with all this. I had thought I had a choice. I had thought no one could really hurt me again. Just this morning, Bill had assured me he would be my protector. I had thought I had some control over what happened to me. I realized I was as powerless as ever. They owned me and kept me by fear and intimidation.

Worst of all, this time around, Brian couldn't save me anymore. Brian couldn't help heal the wounds and tell me how special I was, tell me he loved me. Brian couldn't take me to the beach or the mall or the movies, where I could act like I was his son and everything was normal.

I felt like my heart and mind were broken. I sobbed so hard that my whole body shook. This freaked Tyler out. He turned off the water and put a towel around my shoulders and tried to dry me off. A black curtain was starting to cover my vision, so I sat down and put my head between my legs. The last thing I heard before I passed out was Tyler calling for his dad.

GAY OR NOT?

I woke up in a bed bigger than I've ever seen or imagined. The whole room was incredible. It had its own living room and kitchen and another door, probably leading to the bathroom. While I lay there, I was mentally taking inventory of myself. I could tell where I still hurt from the whipping. My head hurt from all the anxiety and I still had no clothes on. I looked up when the door opened, and Bill walked in. I tried to sit up really quickly, not knowing what was expected of me.

"Lay down, Timmy."

I did as he said, and he sat on the bed next to me.

"Are you okay?"

"Yes."

"You talk in your sleep. Did you know that?"

"No."

"Well, you do. Come with me."

I started to get out of bed and stopped because I had no clothes on.

"Don't be bashful now."

I stood up and still feel a little light-headed. He held my arm to steady me and helped me walk. We went through the door and into the biggest bathroom I'd ever seen. He turned on the lights and stood me in front of the mirror sideways so I could see my backside. "Look, no cuts, no blood, just a few welts. No big deal."

Easy for him to say; it wasn't his body that had just been whipped. What an asshole I thought. I just nodded in agreement; no way was I making him mad twice in one day.

Then he turned me straight at the mirror and asked, "What do you see?"

I just shrugged my shoulders, not knowing what kind of answer he wanted.

He picked up a brush and fixed my messy hair. This was a side of Bill I had never seen before. "Let me tell you what I see—a smart, beautiful kid with blond hair and green eyes. Your body is perfect, and your face is adorable. For right now, I own you. But I promise you, when you're older, I will send you to any college you want to go to. I will help you become anything you want to be. Money will be no object." Then he paused and turned me so I was looking him in the eye. "I was wrong earlier when I said you weren't good enough and you weren't like us. I wasn't always rich. When I was a kid, I was poor like you, so I do understand. But my son doesn't know, nor will he ever know, poverty. That's as much explaining as I'm going to do today."

"Okay." I smiled at him. I understood most of what he'd said. He owned me for now, but he would take care of me later. It was still kind of scary.

"Tyler will be up here soon. But for now, get back to bed."

I climbed back into bed, and he went to the other side and leaned back against the headboard. I looked at the bedside clock and saw that it was past midnight. He saw where I was looking and replied, "Yes, you've been asleep almost seven hours."

No matter how nice he was being, I was still extremely mad at him for what had happened, and I still didn't trust him. I knew I couldn't show either. "You know, Timmy, you talk and answer questions in your sleep. You don't always make sense, but I still learned a lot about you. I love you, and I want you even more than ever."

What a strange comment coming from him. What the hell had I said?

He kissed me on my forehead and turned the TV on for me. Then he left the room.

This day had sucked royally. It was supposed to be a day of fun—a day of helping a friend put together a great party for his friends. Nothing seemed to turn out right for me. It was around 1:30 a.m. when Tyler walked in wearing sweats and an oversize

T-shirt. His hair was wet from a shower or the pool. I didn't know which. He gave me a sad look and said. "I'm so sorry. Please forgive me."

"Why should I?"

"Because I thought Dad gave you the money, kind of buying my friendship. I thought you really didn't like me. You were just acting like it to get the money."

"Tyler, I tried to tell you, but you wouldn't listen to me."

"I know. I'm really sorry. Dad explained everything."

"It's okay."

"So you're not mad?"

I felt tired beyond belief and answered, "No, I'm not mad anymore."

"How do you feel?"

"I'm okay, I guess." It was better to downplay at the moment.

"Does it hurt?"

"No. It's really not that bad." I rolled over to show him, figuring this would make him believe me.

"Shit," That looks like it really hurts" I'm sorry"

"Trust me, Tyler. I've had worse."

"Then what happened in the shower?"

"Sometimes when I'm scared, my mind just shuts down and I kind of freak out then I fall asleep."

"You've done this before?"

"Yeah"

"Did you know you talk in your sleep?"

"Your dad said the same thing. What do I talk about?"

"You don't want to know." Then he crawled next to me in bed.

"What did I say? You have to tell me?"

"Scary stuff, Timmy" I wish I could make your life better." Then he put his arm around me and patted my shoulder.

We both lay back on our pillows and figured it was easier to watch TV than to stay on this subject.

"Promise me one thing, Tyler."

"What's that?"

"That you won't get mad at me like that again"

"I promise."

"How was the party?"

"I'm sorry about that, Timmy; I will make it up to you."

"Well, how was it?"

"It would have been better if you had been there. I didn't have a good time because I was worried about you."

"How was the food?"

"Great!"

"Is there any left? I'm starving. I haven't eaten since dinner last night."

"Why didn't you say anything?"

"I thought we would eat at the mall."

"The caterers took the extra food with them. What do you want to eat?"

"Anything"

"I'll go make you something."

"Can I go too?"

"No. You just rest. Let me do this for you."

About fifteen minutes later, he came back with a piece of chicken, mashed potatoes and gravy, and three slices of pizza. I was so hungry I ate every bit of it. While I ate, Tyler told me more about the party. About seventy-five teenagers, including some of the hottest cheerleaders and the jocks—basically all the popular people—had attended. It was just like I had pictured it would be.

"It sounds like a great party, Tyler."

"I know. I'm sorry."

Then we talked about girls and cars and all the important stuff to boys trying to grow up. We were having a great time until Tyler turned his questions to life at my house.

"I know I already asked you this but why does your mom beat you" I need to know why" "I wanted to say, *so does your dad*" But I couldn't say what I was thinking.

"Yeah"

"Why?"

"Because her dad used to beat her, and his dad used to beat him, and on and on" Tyler, I don't want to talk about my family."

"Why?"

"I just don't."

"It's not fair. You know everything about me."

"I don't know anything about you."

"Yes you do."

Frustrated and wanting this over I asked, "What do you want to know?"

"Why do you make those movies?"

"They made me."

"Who made you?"

"The group"

"Who's the group?"

"I'm not allowed to talk about it."

"Why?"

"The same reason you don't tell me your dad's real name and what he does for a living. Even though I know his name is Robert, I am supposed to call him Bill."

Tyler looked shocked.

I continued, "Tyler, please. I'm ten you're fifteen. You're older and smarter than me. If you make me talk, I am going to end up on a rack somewhere getting the hell beat out of me."

"Timmy, I would never tell on you."

"I know. But whose room is this?"

"Nobody's It's an extra bedroom. Why? Do you think the room is bugged?"

"No. I'm so tired, Tyler. Let's just go to sleep." I rolled to one side of the bed and got comfortable and fell asleep.

I woke up and looked at the clock, and it was 11:00 a.m. I still didn't have my clothes, and I felt stuck in the room. Tyler was still asleep. Then I remembered that Dad and Bill had a meeting at 9:00 a.m. I wondered why Bill hadn't just awakened me up and taken me with him.

About an hour later, Bill walked in and motioned for me to follow him. I was being extra quiet, and he told me not to worry; Tyler could sleep through an earthquake.

I ran to the bathroom and wrapped a towel around my waist. Bill rolled his eyes at me. Instead of going to where my clothes had been left, he took me to the gym, through the locker room where the steam room and Jacuzzi were. Like father, like son, I thought. I felt so powerless; a year ago, this would have freaked me out.

We walked past that stuff and up to a door. Bill handed me the key and told me to open it. It used to be a storage area; it was painted gray and had a concrete floor. It was bigger than my bedroom at home, but it seemed small in this mansion. There were shelves with some clothes folded on it.

"What do you think?" Bill asked me. I was confused because I didn't know what the room was for.

"I think it's nice."

"Good, because this is your space, and those clothes are some of Tyler's that don't fit anymore. No one can get in here but you. You can keep your stuff here if you want, and it will be safe. I know you're afraid to take your money home, and that is smart of you. I know you have money and things at Brian's house that you can't take home. You also have money at Rick and Todd's too. Now you have a place for all that. I gave you your own lockbox to keep your money. Only you will have a key to that. You can come and go as you please."

"Do I have to sleep in here?"

"No, Timmy, it's not a bedroom. It's a storage space. There are plenty of rooms in this house to sleep in."

"Thanks, Bill."

I liked the idea a lot. I had a safe place to keep my money. The guys in the group liked buying us boys stuff. My room at Brian's was packed with electronics and everything a kid could want. They loved to please us and enjoyed seeing us get great presents. Sometimes they would try to outdo each other. But what it all came down to for them was sex. No matter how well they treated you, their ulterior motive was getting from you whatever it took to give them sexual pleasure. And nowadays, this was getting more and more complicated. So they used blackmail and guilt, anything and everything that could work. They knew not to keep a kid miserable, or one day he would break.

Show a little love and concern, buy presents and give money, make the kids feel important—these things kept kids in the group until the adults were done with them. The guys were full of compliments and made us kids feel like we were a part of an elite group. All this messed with our heads so bad that we kids ended up protecting their dark, destructive, secret world. Wondering why I was so quiet, Bill asked, "What are you thinking?"

I was caught off guard. I wasn't used to people caring. "I was wondering where my clothes are."

"They are on the shelf, clean and folded." He walked back to the Jacuzzi and undressed and got in. "Join me." It was said as a request, but there were no options in this world.

I took my towel off and had trouble getting in quickly because it was so hot. I could tell this excited Bill, and I wanted to distract him with conversation. "Did you meet with my dad today?"

"Yes, I did. I liked him, and he's going to give me a price on a couple of jobs. I could tell he liked me and was impressed that you were Tyler's friend. It wasn't anything he said, just the way he acted. Timmy, you did some talking last night in your sleep."

"Bill, I'm sorry, you have to believe me. I don't know what I said."

"Well, I am sorry for mistreating you yesterday. I shouldn't have scared you out of your mind like that. You told me what Rick and Todd did to you."

"Oh shit, I did?"

"Yes, you did. I know they gave you a lot of money. Where is it?"

"They still have it."

"You mean you went through that hell, and they still have your money?"

"Yes."

"Don't worry; I will get it back for you."

Then he moved closer to me, and I knew that our conversation was over. He was very experienced and wanted to give, not just take. Each man had his own fantasy, and somehow, we boys figured it out and played our part. The guys never knew how much was acting; if they did, it would have hurt their egos.

I looked up and saw someone watching us through a crack in the door. It was Anna. She didn't turn away during any of it. If I could see her, so could Bill. It was strange. No one seemed to care but me, and I hated the idea of her seeing this.

Bill and I took a shower, and I could finally get dressed. He handed me two envelopes, explaining one was the money I had given back to him in the car. I opened them and counted the money in front of Bill. I was very pleased and smiled I took fifty dollars and put the rest in the lockbox and locked the door. When I came out, Bill was waiting for me.

"Is everything okay?"

"Yes."

"Then I'll take you home."

In the car, he reminded me that he would collect all my money from Brian and from Rick. I was worried that Bill would make Brian mad. I was surprised that Brian had made no effort to get a hold of me or see me. That wasn't like him.

Bill dropped me off at home. Dad and Tommy were washing the car in the driveway. I thanked Bill and opened the door just as dad came over to talk to Bill.

I picked up a rag to help, and Tommy yelled, "We don't need your help."

I threw the rag back in the bucket and went in the house. Mom was cleaning and in a really good mood. She said, "Timmy, I need some milk from the store. Would you ride your bike to the store for me?"

"Sure, Mom"

I got on my bike to leave, and as I was passing Dad, he asked, "Where do you think you're going?"

"Getting some milk for Mom"

"Did you have a good time at Bill's house?"

"Yeah, it was great."

"They sure are rich," Dad said, and I smiled in agreement.

When I got to the store, I bought two boxes of candy also and made sure Mom and Dad saw them. I wanted to show a reason to start having money. I told them I was going to start selling the candy at school like Tommy did.

When Tommy heard this, he got mad. Dad yelled at him to shut up, explaining that we went to different schools so I couldn't steal any of his customers. Tommy stormed off into his room.

On Monday, I rode my bike to school and took one box of candy bars with me. I had no plans of selling them. I gave them away to my friends. This made me even more popular, and that never hurt. At lunch, my table was even more crowded.

Denny was sitting next to me, and he was really upset, so I asked, "What's wrong?"

"The boys in the sixth grade are picking on me."

"Why?"

"I don't know. They keep calling me names like fag, fairy, and queer."

"Why"

"I don't know" They say I like boys instead of girls. I don't know what I did to make these guys mad at me."

"Don't worry. It will be all right." I put my arm around him.

Just then, a couple of the sixth graders walked up. "See, I told you they were fairies," one said.

"You're a bunch of butt-fucking morons I yelled! And the best you can come up with is fairies. Is that what you think I am?"

"Yeah he says"

"If I'm a fairy then, poof, you're a piece of shit"

They didn't know how to come back from that one, and they walked away mad.

At recess I told Denny to stay with me, and we started playing dodge ball with a group of guys. It wasn't long before about ten sixth graders showed up and picked up where they'd left off at lunch. The name-calling went from bad to worse, and I was doing my best to suck it up and hope they would just leave. This surprised my friends because they thought I would get into a fight with anyone if I would fight the school bully and win. I was smart enough to know I didn't always win.

I was scared and hiding it well, but a guy can only take so much. I grabbed the ball and set it down and faced the group. "Whose ass do I have to kick to get you guys to shut up?!"

They were surprised at this threat. They were brave at name-calling younger kids but weren't sure what to do now that I had called them on it.

So I started to point at each guy asking, "Is it you? Who is it?"

They looked at each other, and soon enough, they all walked away.

Ms. Right always gave the class ten minutes of quiet time after recess. Most kids hated having to be quiet and still like that. I enjoyed it. But today I was really disturbed about the names the older kids called me and Denny. These were all words I knew from the group, but no one had called me names like that. I didn't know if they thought I was gay or just using it as a way of riding us younger kids. I was confused and knew I needed to talk to someone.

I lay my head back on the desk, and without realizing it, I fell asleep. I jumped when I heard a loud bang!

Ms. Right asked. "Are you sleeping?"

My face was wet with drool, and I wiped it answering, "No, Ms. Right."

The whole class couldn't help but laugh.

"What page are we on?"

I didn't know which book she was even talking about. "I don't know."

She just turned and walked back to the front of the room.

I looked over at Denny and said, "Thanks a lot for the warning."

He just looked at me confused.

The school bell finally rang, and Denny found me at the bike rack and asked if I wanted to come over. I told him that I had plans, and I began my long ride to Tyler's house. It was cool outside, but at least it wasn't raining this time. When I got to the front gates, I used the access number and let myself in. I went in the back way, and when I got near the kitchen I yelled for Tyler.

Anna heard me and called me over to her. She said, "Timmy, I didn't know you were coming over today."

"I didn't either. Is Tyler here?"

"He'll be here in about fifteen or twenty minutes. Are you hungry?"

"Yeah"

"Well sit down for a minute, and I will fix you a sandwich." She made me a huge turkey and cheese and a big glass of milk. Then she sat down across from me and said, "I didn't mean to spy on you yesterday."

I shrugged my shoulders and blushed. I had forgotten about it already.

"Are you mad at me?"

"No. I forgot about it. Why did you watch?"

"I don't know. I just couldn't turn away."

"You know Bill saw you."

"How do you know?"

"Anna, you were standing right there. How could he not see you?"

"Did he say anything to you?"

"No."

"Did you tell him?"

"No."

"Then how do you know?"

"I could see you easily, so I figured he could too."

"Were you embarrassed that I watched?"

"Yeah!"

"Sorry."

Then Tyler walked in. and says, "Timmy, you're here?" he said. "I was just thinking about you."

Anna spoke up. "He gets a greeting, and you just ignore me like I'm not even here."

"Sorry, Anna," Tyler replied. Then he spoke to her in Spanish, and she answered back and smiled. "Come with me," Tyler said. I followed him up to his room. "I'm hanging out with some friends in a little while. Do you want to come?" He started changing into some other clothes.

I look away and answered, "No, but thanks anyways."

"Why did you come over?"

"I need to ask you a few questions."

"Okay."

"Am I a homosexual?"

"What?" He laughed.

"Please, Tyler; I don't think it's funny."

"Why are you asking?"

"Because some kids at school were calling me names"

"What did you do?"

"I called them names back and offered to fight them. They walked away."

"Timmy, only you can answer that question."

"Are you?"

"No. I like both boys and girls. You're the only boy I have been with."

"Is your dad?"

"No. He likes women, and he's just a pervert."

"What about Brian?"

"What I can tell is that he's a flamer."

"What's that?"

"It's obvious that he's gay."

"I don't know what I am. I like girls even though I've never been with one."

"Never"

"Tyler, I'm just a kid"

"I'll tell you what when I have another party I'll set you up"

"Thanks."

"But really, Timmy, don't worry about it. I don't think you are."

"Why?"

"You just don't act like it. Hey, I got to go. Will you be all right?"

"Yeah, see you later."

I walked down to the kitchen and thanked Anna for the food then headed home. Going home was easier because it was more downhill than uphill.

After talking to Tyler, I felt better. I got home early and put my bike away and listened at the door.

I walked in nice and quiet and headed for my room. My bedroom door was open, and that was never a good sign. It looked like a tornado had hit it—a tornado named Linda, my mom. She had piled everything she could on the floor in the middle of my room. All my drawers were emptied out. My closet was emptied, my sheets and blankets torn off the bed. It had been a while since she had done this to me. I got scared. This meant that she was looking for someone to beat.

I turned around, and there she was, blocking the only exit. She was holding a lighter and a huge syringe. I had found this syringe and used it for a water gun; it was one you used in the kitchen. That was all she needed to find a reason to be mad.

"You're smoking and doing drugs!" she accused.

She knew the syringe wasn't even the right kind, but it fit the mood she was in. She swung a broomstick around, and it hit me upside the head. I went straight to my knees. The next one caught the back of my head, and I balled up on the ground covering my head with my hands as best I could. She screamed and swung. I screamed and begged her to stop. I lost count of the hits; it went on forever. I heard her mumbling something about my brother, and she stormed out of the room.

I lay there awhile, afraid she was coming right back. When she didn't, I knew it was time to start cleaning my room. This was a huge task because I had to put everything away and make my room perfect, or she would do this all over again. I worked on it for a couple of hours, doing the best job I could.

I heard my brother come home and knew what he was in for. In only a few moments, I could hear his screams. A little while later, my mom threw open the door and started checking everything each dresser drawer, my closet, under my bed, my covers on my bed. Thank God, she was satisfied.

She tells me that dinner was ready, and I headed to the table. There wasn't a place set for my dad, so I guessed he was out of town. Our plates were made already, and you could tell she had put a lot of thought into tonight. She'd purposely picked the foods we hated so she could watch us struggle. My brother and I looked at each other and knew we were in for a long night of getting slapped and food shoved down our throats.

An hour later, our cheeks were bright red from her hand, and she was taking turns force-feeding each of us. When she'd had enough of this fun, she told us to clean up the kitchen. She was going to bed because we had given her a headache. We were just glad to see her go. We got the kitchen cleaned. Tommy went to bed, and I took a bath and soaked my new wounds.

We both got up early and out of the house the next morning. The day was uneventful, and I wasn't looking forward to school getting out. It was Tuesday, and I knew Rick or Todd would be picking me up. I was walking with my head down, the weight of the world on my shoulders. Last night with mom had been pretty bad, and I never looked forward to going over to Rick and Todd's house. Little did I know, my day could get worse? I wasn't paying attention to my surroundings, and before I knew it, I had walked into a trap.

The sixth graders must have felt humiliated by what I'd said to them yesterday because they even brought some older kids with them. I had started down a shortcut on my way to meet Todd after school, and when I looked up; I could see a couple of the kids at the end waiting for me. I turned around planning to backtrack. More kids were blocking my way behind me. The only way out was sideways. I tried to jump a wall, and one of the boys pulled me back. There were at least ten kids, and four of them were in high school. I didn't have a chance.

One kid pinned my arms behind my back, forcing me to stand up and leaving my face and body unprotected. They took turns punching me for quite a while. I was a mess. My nose was bloodied; my lips were busted open. Tears and blood ran into my eyes.

Then I heard one of the boys say, "Now I am going to give you the one thing that made you famous." He kicked me in the nuts. The guy behind me let go, and I fell to the ground crying out in pain. The guys were laughing and decided this was enough and they left.

I lay there moaning for a little while until I could stand up and walk to Thrifty's. Todd wasn't there so I used the pay phone to call Tyler. "Can you have someone pick me up?" I asked.

"Why?"

"I just got jumped."

"I'm leaving"

"Can you call your dad for me? Please, Tyler, I need him."

"Okay. Where are you?"

I told him and sat down in the phone booth and tried not to cry. A few people walked by and looked concerned but didn't want to get involved. Tyler showed up in a really nice Mercedes with a couple of his friends. Tyler and a friend grabbed an arm and helped me get in the car. I knew it was bad when one of the guys suggested I go to a hospital.

"No. Just take me to your dad, Tyler. He'll know what to do."

I just sat there leaning against one of the guys, hurting too badly to sit up straight. Tyler called his dad from the phone booth.

"Dad will meet us at the house."

I closed my eyes on the ride. When I opened them, I saw Bill reaching for me, and he carried me into the house. I put my head on his shoulder and couldn't stop the tears. "You're safe now," Bill said.

It was easy to believe him. He cleaned me up; wrapped me in a soft, white robe; and put me on his bed and covered me. I must have fallen asleep for a little while. I woke up on this huge, extremely comfortable bed with a mirror on the ceiling above it. I heard Bill's voice, and he was on the other side talking on the phone. I crawled over to him and lay my head in his lap. I could tell he liked this, and he began to stroke my hair as he kept talking. I looked into the mirror above me, and my face didn't look as bad as it felt. I'd taken a lot of punches to the chest and stomach, and it was a little hard to breathe. But what hurt the most was my privates.

FRESH MEAT

Tyler came home from a friend's house and checked in on me. "How are you doing?" he asked.

"Better."

He looked my face and chest over, "Boy, you have a lot of bruises."

I turned to Bill and asked, "Did you call Rick and Todd?"

"Yes. Don't worry. Everything is taken care of. Rick and Todd are bringing Carlos and Troy over here."

I must have looked shocked. Bill knew what I was afraid of. "Don't worry, Timmy, they aren't coming for that."

I tried to sit up but felt too dizzy. It wasn't long before everyone showed up. Everyone was in Bill's room talking and catching up on what was new when Bill ordered everyone but Rick out so he could see what the damage was.

As he was doing an exam, Rick asked, "How do you make so many people mad at you?" When he saw my privates he said, "Boy that had to hurt" You'll need to protect those better "These guys must have hit like girls because this is nothing compared to the last time you got jumped. Bill left the room I'd been hoping that part was only a joke.

"Timmy, you'll be fine," Rick said. He wrote me a note for school. "Don't let your parents see this." Just take it to the office"

Bill came back so I covered myself now that Rick was done.

When the guys came back in the room, they were a lot quieter.

I asked, "What's wrong with you guys?"

Rick answered, "We have some bad news for you."

"What?"

"You've noticed how Brian hasn't been around lately."

"Yeah"

"This is hard to tell you, but . . . Brian has a new kid."

I shouldn't have been shocked, but I was. I knew when I left that I would be replaced. But having to hear that it had happened and then having them all watch how I handled it made it even harder. I couldn't stop the tears from running down my face.

"Carlos, how long have you known?"

"I just found out." I knew he was lying.

"Why didn't you tell me?"

"I don't know. I don't even like the kid."

All kinds of thoughts went through my mind—like ways of getting back into Brian's life and getting rid of the new kid. I was remembering good times and special moments. I cried even harder, and it made the pain worse. This was one of the worst days of my life. First I got jumped, and then my heart got broken.

Carlos lies down next to me and put his arm around me. I turned into him and cried even harder. Troy went to the other side of me and rubbed my back. Tyler sat down on the end of the bed. The men left the room, realizing there was nothing they could do.

"So that's why I haven't seen you around here?" I asked Carlos.

"Probably"

"Does Brian bring him over to your house?"

"No. He's not ready yet," Carlos answered.

Tyler looked back and forth between us with a confused look.

"So he hasn't been to a party yet."

"No!"

"Does the group like him?"

"Fresh meat, Timmy, of course they do."

"Is that why Bill has taken me over?"

"Probably"

"What are you guys talking about?" Tyler asked.

Carlos gave him a look that said, *Don't interrupt.*

I've met him," Troy offered. "He's nothing like you. You're a lot cuter."

"Brian tried to pass him off as you after you left," Carlos added, "but the guys still wanted you back."

I was ready for this conversation to end now. I asked, "Carlos, will you go get me some clothes? Troy, will you help me up?" I sat up really slowly, moving the ice pack and setting it next to me. Troy picked it up and started playing with it. I warned him, "Troy if you knew where that has been, you wouldn't be playing with it."

"Where has it been?" Troy asked looking confused.

"Cooling my nuts," I laughed.

He ran into the bathroom and washed his hands.

Now that I was sitting up, I had a chance to look around Bill's room. It had its own living room, twice as large as the other room. There was a liquor bar on the other side of a pool table and a dart set. The bathroom was fit for a king.

Carlos came back with some clothes and helped me get dressed. I could have done it by myself, but Carlos always assumed this role, especially when I was hurt. I had never noticed him act that way with any of the other guys.

Carlos saw my back and asked, "Did those guys use sticks on you?"

"No."

"Then your mother got a hold of you, didn't she?"

"Yeah, last night"

"Did you tell Bill?"

"What for"

"Maybe he can have her killed."

We all laughed and walked out of the room. We searched for the men until we found them in the garage admiring Bill's car collection.

"Good, Timmy," Bill said, "you're out of bed."

I smiled up at him.

"I bet you're starved. Let's go get a good meal."

The whole group loaded up in a couple of cars, and Bill led us up a winding road to the top of a hill. It was a steak house and very crowded at this time. One of the hostesses recognized Bill and went to get the manager. The manager walked up to our group and personally escorted us to the best table. It had a view that overlooked the city. I looked back at the line of people waiting and could see some were really upset. This was so cool. Bill slipped the manager some money in a handshake. My experience with eating out was limited to fast food places and my parents ordering for me. I saw the prices on the menu, and looking around, realized the only people surprised were Troy and me.

The waiter arrived to take our orders and started with Bill first then moved around the table. I was the last one and didn't know what to say.

The waiter looked at me questioningly, "Sir?"

Carlos turned to Bill and said, "Brian always orders for him."

Bill smiled and placed my order.

The men were all talking and enjoying a chance to visit. Tyler and Carlos were talking up a storm.

I turned to Troy, "How have you been?"

"Now that your back, I'm great."

"I don't get it, Troy. How do I make a difference?'

"You're kidding right? You're the only one who gives a shit. No one else cares, not Nick or Carlos. By the way, did you know that Nick was gone?"

"Gone where?"

"He moved with his family to San Francisco. Richard and I helped them move. I was glad to see him go."

"Me too" He was an ass."

"Anyway, things are better now. Maybe over Christmas break we can hang out?"

"That would be great"

"You know there is a party Saturday?" Troy says me.

"Did you have to remind me? Will the new kid be there?"

Troy shrugged, and the waiters arrived with our food. It smelled delicious, and I was starving. We all ate until we were stuffed, and everyone was smiling when we left.

Bill drove me home and walked me to the door. "Go get your mother," he told me.

I opened the door and called out, "Mom," real loud. She was behind the door waiting for me. When she saw Bill standing there, she was embarrassed at being caught by an adult. She stepped forward and started talking to him.

I thanked Bill and headed to my room while she was distracted. I really wanted to hide and listen, but there was no way I could do it without getting caught so I just went to my room and went to bed.

About twenty minutes later, I heard the front door close, and Mom came straight to my room. I tensed up, not sure why she was there. She left the light off and came over and kissed me. "I love you, Timmy," she said. I answered back, "I love you too, Mom." I never knew what to expect from her.

I rode my bike to school the next morning and gave the school secretary the note Rick had written. She accepted it with no question. Everyone was staring at me because the story of what had happened the previous day had made it all around school. I was quiet and kept to myself. Everyone probably thought it was because of getting beat up, but my mind was on Brian.

As I sat in class, Denny finally said to me, "Nice shiner."

"What?"

"Everyone is talking about how Randy kicked your ass."

"Like hell he did"

"What do you mean?"

"It was Randy and a dozen of his friends, most of them from high school. They jumped me. Randy is a coward."

Just then I heard my name over the intercom telling me to come to the front office.

A kid named Mike said, "Oh, poor Timmy."

I stopped in front of his desk and said, "I'll lay you out! Just say another word."

"That will be enough, Timmy," Ms. Right said. "Get to the office."

When I got to the office Principle Davies showed me a chair to sit in and asked me, "Timmy, is there anything you want to tell me?"

"No, sir"

"You don't have anything at all you want to tell me?"

"No, sir"

"I heard you got into a fight yesterday."

"If you want to call it that"

"Excuse me, little man, I have a paddle right here. If you keep it up, it will have your name on it. Do you understand me?"

"Yes, sir"

"So tell me what happened yesterday."

"I was jumped"

"Jumped? You mean you were in a fight."

"No. I was jumped."

"By whom"

"Randy, Cory, Mike, Stewart, and some other boys. I don't know their names. Most of them were from high school."

"How many were there?"

"Ten or twelve I'm not sure."

"Timmy, this isn't the story I've been told."

He called the secretary and had her call in some of the boys. He called them into his office one at a time. I guess they had made a pact not to tell, but Mr. Davies was very intimidating. By the time he was done with them he had a total of eleven names.

Mr. Davies apologized to me. "I'm really sorry about what happened. When something like this happens, you have to tell me so I can protect you and the other kids. Do you want me to call your parents?"

"No, please don't."

"Why?"

"My family doesn't believe in fighting, and I will get spanked," I lied, knowing my mom didn't need an excuse to hit me, but I didn't want to give her one either.

"Okay, go back to class and I will take care of this."

I knew he couldn't make it right or protect me. I also knew those high school kids were going to be madder than hell at me. I knew paybacks were a bitch. I wanted school to go by real slow today because I knew they would be looking for me.

When the bell rang, I ran out to my bike. I planned to head a different way home than usual, except I was going nowhere on my bike. My tires were slashed. I carried my bike back toward the office so I could use the phone.

Mr. Davies saw me and asked, "What's wrong, Timmy?"

"Someone slashed my tires."

"Who do you think did it?"

I just looked at him kind of funny, wondering if this guy could be that dense. "I'll give you eleven guesses."

"No way, Timmy, those boys are scared. They won't ever touch you again." He was the only one who seemed convinced.

"Can I use the phone?"

"Sure."

I called Bill's office and explained my situation. He told me he was in a meeting and would have someone pick me up. He also warned me not to leave the school grounds. I did one better than that. While I was waiting, I made sure that anyone in the office could see me standing outside. It wasn't long before a truck with three teens in the front and a bunch in the back pulled up and yelled, "What's wrong, kid? Do you need a ride?"

"No, I have one."

"Come on, kid, get in. Let's get this over with."

"Yeah, get in, like it would be a fair fight—a truckload of high school kids against one fourth grader. What's fair about that?"

"No, kid, it will be just you and me."

"Yeah, like yesterday—eleven against one. No thanks. I have a ride coming."

"Look, kid, get in and I'll make it easy on you. I promise."

One of the kids in the back jumped out and took my bike and put it in the back of the truck. Another kid from the front got out and grabbed me, saying, "Get it over with."

I got stuck between two kids, and I was scared to death. On the other hand, I didn't want to live in fear every day waiting for them to find me and beat me up. I was sizing up all my enemies that I could see, and there was something about the driver. I felt I could trust him if I had to.

We drove for a while and ended up on a dirt road looking at a sign that said "No Trespassing." Everyone piled out of the truck, excited about what was about to happen. I got out slowly, and a big kid grabbed me from behind and walked me over to where they were all waiting. I'm glad he grabbed me because my knees were so weak I don't think I could have walked. I even thought about crawling on my knees and asking for mercy. My body just couldn't take another beating like that again so soon.

The driver stood in front of me and said, "I can't believe you had the guts to get in the truck like that. Are you stupid or something?" I hadn't felt like I had a choice in the matter. I was scared and had tears in my eyes, but I wasn't crying. "I'll tell you what. You can pick anyone here to fight."

I looked around and they were all definitely a lot bigger than me. But the driver was the biggest of them all. I felt that if anyone would show me mercy, it would be him. So I looked him dead in the eye.

"Are you picking me?" he asked, surprised.

I nodded and everyone laughed. "Are you stupid or something?"

At this point, I figured he was right. I was stupid. But I had to hope I'd read him correctly.

The other kids acted like a crazy mob, yelling things like, "Kevin, kick his ass. Beat the shit out of him."

All I could think was that I was in the middle of nowhere, with a mob that wanted me dead. Kevin could see the fear building in me. He yelled for them all to shut up. They did, and he said, "This must be your lucky day, kid. You were right to pick me."

Someone from the group yelled, "If you won't fight him, I will."

Kevin asked, "You want to fight him?"

"Hell yes!"

"Then you have to fight me first."

Everyone got quiet, taking in this new turn of events. "That's what I thought, you pussy! Get your asses in the truck "They all did what he said. Kevin turned to me and said, "Good luck." Then he gives me directions so I could make my way out of there. As they pulled away, the guys in the back continued to yell obscenities at me.

I couldn't believe how lucky I was. There was a part of me that was afraid he would change his mind and turn around to finish what he'd started. After walking about half an hour, I found the spot where they'd thrown my bike out of the truck. The wheels were bent badly, the handlebars were broken, and it was completely wrecked. I just left it behind some bushes because it wasn't worth carrying. It took another half hour of walking to finally hit pavement.

I didn't know which way to go. It seemed I was in some kind of canyon. There were a lot of cars going by, so I decided the only way out was hitchhiking. It was my first time, and it didn't take long for a guy to pull over.

The driver was in his forties, bald, and overweight. He was really hairy like a caveman. "Kid, get in," he said.

I opened the passenger door and jumped in.

"Where are you going?"

I told him where I lived, and he laughed. "You're hitchhiking in the wrong direction. You need to go on the other side of the road."

I thanked him and got out of the car and asked, "Is there a pay phone anywhere around here?"

"Just up the road at the Texaco station."

"Can you take me there?"

"Sure."

"What are you doing out here anyways?"

\He probably didn't want the whole story, but he got it anyways.

I called Bill's house, and Tyler answered the phone. "Where the hell are you?"

"I don't know. I'm at a gas station. Where's your dad?"

"He and some guys from work are out looking for you. He's really worried about you. What street are you on?"

"I don't know."

"What is the phone number?"

I read it to him off the phone.

"Now go ask the gas station attendant what the address is."

I did and walked back to the phone and waited for it to ring.

I picked it up when it rang, and I gave Bill the address. Then he said, "I swear, Timmy, if you're not there this time, I'm going to kill you. Don't move! Do you hear me?"

"Yes, sir" I'd known he would be mad, but I hadn't imagined it would be this bad. He pulled up, and I got into the car.

"Where the hell have you been? Are you all right?"

"Yes."

"I told you to wait at the school for a ride."

"I know."

"Where the hell have you been? Do you know how much money I have lost these last two days because of you?" He kept yelling and cussing, and I sat there feeling defeated.

I saw the road where I had left my bike and said, "Turn here."

"Why?' he asked as he made the turn.

"My bike is over there."

He stopped the car and got out, and when he saw how trashed it was, he said, "What the hell! This bike isn't worth fixing. Leave it. All right, Timmy, now tell me what happened." Finally he wasn't mad anymore.

I told him everything from the time the kids had forced me in the truck in front of the school.

"Well, Timmy, this stuff just seems to keep happening to you. You are the unluckiest kid I know. What are you going to do about a bike?"

"I have money. I'll buy a new one."

"Yes, you sure do. But who is going to pay me for my time and the money I lost."

"I will."

"It would take you a lifetime, but I think I know how you can work it off." Then he laughed.

It was around 5:30, so Bill took me home. My luck was changing because Mom was in a good mood.

(Next Saturday) was the big party, and Bill picked me up at our usual meeting place at Thrifty's at 7:00 a.m. When I got in, I asked Bill, "Where's Tyler?"

"Has there ever been a party that Tyler has been to?"

"No."

"That's right. We don't talk to him about them, and he never knows what goes on at them. Do you understand?'

"Yes, sir"

"Good. Now you have plenty of time before the party. You can swim, play in the game room, anything you want to do, but you have to keep yourself busy. I have a lot of work to catch up on. Stay out of the way of everyone setting up."

First I went to the weight room and worked out like Brian had showed me. I thought I did pretty well. Bill had two pools, one inside and one outside. I had never been to the one inside, so when I found it and checked the temperature I decided to get in. I didn't have a bathing suit, and soon enough, I wouldn't be allowed to wear clothes, so I just got in.

I swam around on an inflatable ball for a while, thinking about what might lie ahead. First I wondered if Brian would show up. Then I was kind of worried because it was my first party back, and I didn't know how the guys would act toward me. I didn't know if they would still be mad at me for leaving.

I felt someone watching me. When I looked around, I found Brian had snuck in and sat quietly on the diving board. I had been so deep in thought I hadn't even noticed. I wanted to yell his name and swim right to him, but I stopped myself. I remembered he had traded me in for a newer, younger boy. So I cleared my throat and acted nonchalant. "What are you doing here?" I asked.

"I thought we should talk before the party, so it wouldn't be awkward."

"Is he going to be here?"

"No."

"Why?"

"Because he's not ready"

"What's his name?"

"Joey."

"Do I know him?"

"Yes, he's in my class." I turned and swam away, and he called after me, "Timmy, we have to talk."

"No, we don't! Please, just go away."

"No, not until we talk."

He undressed, jumped in the pool, and came toward me.

"I don't want to swim with you"

He skillfully cornered me in the shallow end. I turned to get out, but he grabbed my foot.

"Let me go!"

Brian answered, "No," and pulled me back in.

Tears ran down my cheeks, and my heart pounded so hard my chest hurt. My feelings were crushed, and I cried as I said, "I thought when I moved you were letting me go to protect me. But that wasn't it, was it? You wanted to replace me. I don't live that far away, we could have still seen each other. But you were sick of me."

"No, that's not true."

"Really, which kid did you say it is? Let me guess, Joey—the one who sits in the front row?"

"Yes."

"I knew it."

"What do you mean by that?"

"I picked him out even before I left."

"Really, why"

"I could see the way you looked at him."

"How's that"

"The same way you used to look at me. Now go away!"

He still had me cornered, "We have to talk this out."

"Why?"

"I don't want there to be hard feelings toward me or Joey."

"Fine, no hard feelings, and by the way, I want my money back."

"I already gave it to Bill. Are you mad at me?"

"Yeah, I'm mad and hurt. You made me cry. It hurt worse than any beating my mom ever gave me."

"I'm really sorry. If I could take it back, I would."

"You can send him away."

"No, I can't, Timmy."

"You could if you wanted to."

"I want you to meet Joey."

"I already met him."

"Did you like him?"

"I guess."

"So then you'll be nice to him?"

"Brian, what difference does it make?"

"It matters to me. I still love you, Timmy."

I said, "Fine," and rolled my eyes.

Brian got out of the pool and dressed. He left without saying anything else to me. I didn't want him to leave. I wanted him to change his mind and take me back. It was killing me that he didn't want me back. I wondered what that kid had that I didn't. Then it dawned on me—he was innocent still. The irony of this whole mess was that Brian had stolen my innocence, shared me with others, and then dropped me for someone new and unused.

I got out of the pool, got dressed, and went to Tyler's room. I turned on the stereo and lay down on the bed to relax for a while. I wanted to get back at Brian, but I didn't know how to. I wanted to hurt him like he'd hurt me. I fell asleep plotting revenge and wondering if I could carry any of it through.

I woke up to Troy shaking my shoulder and calling my name, saying, "Timmy, it's time."

Groggily I answered, "Time for what?"

"The party and you better get ready."

"What do I have to do to get ready?"

"Have you looked in the mirror?" he said and smirked.

"No," I answered sarcastically.

"Did you brush your teeth?" Troy continued to hound me.

"What are you, my mother?"

"If I say yes, can I beat the shit out of you?"

I couldn't help but smile at that. I knew I sure couldn't argue with it.

While I was brushing my teeth and fixing my hair, I said to Troy, "I'm a little scared. All the guys were pissed off at me for leaving, even though it wasn't my fault. Bill said there would be a price to pay."

"Well, Timmy, I don't know about all that, but I do know this party is about you."

"It is?"

"Yeah, but trust me, you have nothing to worry about."

"What do you mean?" Somehow this reassurance coming from Troy didn't help me at all. He was at the mercy of the guys just like I was.

"Follow me." I did.

Troy opened the bedroom door and Bill was standing on the other side of it waiting for us. He had a blindfold in his hands, only one—for me. He told me to put it on, and now I was really scared.

Bill asked, "Can you see anything?"

"No."

"Good, don't touch it."

Bill grabbed one arm and Troy grabbed the other. Every bad experience from my past is going through my head. My heart was pounding, and I was getting hot.

Troy whispered in my ear, "Timmy, nothing bad is going to happen to you."

We reached the bottom of the stairs and walked through the house to the back door that led to the pool. Even though I was blindfolded, I knew where I was. At the back door, Bill took off my blindfold, and I heard a chorus voices yell, "Surprise!"

All the guys were there, and behind them was a banner saying, "Welcome Back." A bunch of gifts sat on a table. Bill took me to a brand-new ten-speed bike and said, "We all chipped in since you lost your last bike."

"This is the coolest bike ever!" I was so surprised it was hard for all this to register in my brain. I thought the guys would punish me big-time, but instead they gave me a party with gifts included. As I opened my presents, I was sure to show how much I appreciated the gift.

There were times in the past when the guys had done extra special things for us boys. Carlos told me that, at the last party when

Nick was leaving, they were really good to him. After the presents, it was time to get in the pool. Carlos, Troy, and I stripped down and ran for the pool. The men stayed in a group and seemed to be discussing something important.

Troy asked Carlos, "What's going on?"

"It's about the new boy," Carlos answered.

"What about him?" I asked.

"Those who have met him don't think he is a good candidate for the group," Carlos explained.

I asked, "What do you think?"

Carlos replied, "I don't know. It's not like they are going to ask us for our opinions."

Since we couldn't do anything about it, we began to play Marco Polo.

The guys had a good reason to thoroughly discuss any new kids. Carlos had told me a story of something that had happened before I came into the group. A new kid that they had brought to a party went home and told his parents about it. They went to the police and an investigation began, but there was no way to prove it and no evidence to back it up. It sounded so outrageous that it was hard for any adults to believe him. Most of the men in the group were rich or powerful, or both. Since the investigation, they changed locations, and instead of having the parties at night, they got together in the day.

The meeting broke up, and the guys joined us in the pool for some games of volleyball. The men played hard against each other, and the competition was tough. But they always cut us kids some slack, and it didn't matter if we made mistakes. Some of the guys just skipped the games altogether and hung out in the Jacuzzi.

After about five games and a winning team were established, most of the guys left the pool. A few stayed behind, and I was surprised that one of them was Brian. He swam over to me and asked if I wanted to do flips off his shoulders. He knew how much I loved to do that.

I answered, "Not with you."

This hurt his feelings, and he got out of the pool. I got what I wanted, more distance between us.

Roger got in the pool and got in my face and said, "Timmy that was cold!"

"No, Roger, not being invited to your house or Brian's because of a new kid is cold!"

"That's bullshit, and you know it. You can come over to my house anytime."

"But I can't go over to Brian's, can I?"

"Did Brian say that?"

"No."

"Then don't put words in his mouth. He loves you and cares a great deal about you."

I turned around and got out of the pool and wrapped a towel around me. Bill was in the Jacuzzi with some other guys, and I went and sat next to him and put my feet in the water.

When there was silence, I said, "Bill thanks for the party."

"You're welcome."

"The bike is really cool."

"Good, I hoped you'd like it. You'll be able to get around faster now."

I knew my parents would believe any story I told them about the bike. I figured I would tell them that I traded my bike and some money for it. I also knew all the other presents I got today would need to stay at Bill's house. I was used to that. I told Bill what had just been said between me and Brian and Roger. I needed to hear his advice.

"What should I do?"

The other guys in the Jacuzzi were listening now.

"What do you want to do?"

"I want to tell them to go to hell!"

The other guys laughed at my answer.

"Timmy, I know Brian and his intentions were good. He didn't make you leave so he could replace you. At that time, he felt the best thing was for you to leave the group."

This put a different spin on it for me. "Do I need to apologize?"

"Yes, I think you do."

I sat there for a while, thinking of all the reasons why I shouldn't apologize, but I knew I had to. By now the guys were back to talking about important adult stuff. I looked around for Brian and found him sitting at a table talking to Roger.

I walked up to him and said, "Brian, I'm sorry. I shouldn't be mad at you. My feelings were hurt. Roger, I'm sorry. I meant no disrespect." I didn't want Roger pissed off at me because he still picked me up once in a while to go to Rick and Todd's house. They both just sat staring at me, and I turned to walk away.

"Timmy, I accept your apology," Brian said

With that taken care of, I went to swim some more. They would be cooking soon, and we boys would fix our plates and eat later. They felt it was better for us to perform on an empty stomach instead of a full one. Maybe they thought we would look fat if we ate. Some of them should look in the mirror because they were already overweight. I knew I could eat all I wanted, and I would still look lean. We boys went into the Jacuzzi while they ate, and we knew our time to start was soon. We joked and horsed around, and no one seemed nervous. I acted like I wasn't, but deep down, I was scared.

They called for us to get out, and it was time to get started. They had us put baby oil on each other; this seemed to be one of their favorite things. I didn't mind because it made having sex with them easier later on. They wanted us to wrestle each other and determine a winner. I was the smallest, but if I tried really hard I might be able to beat Troy.

We went first and somehow Troy knocked me down and pinned me before I fought back. I asked for a rematch and was surprised that Bill said yes. The men loved it. I got ready to defend myself this time and felt sure I could do better. It was an exact repeat. I was down and pinned before I knew what happened.

The next matchup was Carlos and Troy. He was almost as good as Carlos. Their match lasted a couple of minutes, and they were both out of breath. Once again, Carlos was the reigning champion. Since I was the loser I had to service both of the guys. I was embarrassed, but because they were teenagers, it didn't take long for me to get results. Since Troy lost to Carlos, I had a chance to be on the receiving end.

By the time we were all done, the men were going nuts. I don't think I could remember a time when they were in such a frenzy.

After that was over, we boys got in the shower and got the oil off our bodies. Then we were starving and finally allowed to eat our food.

We never discussed what we had just been through. In our crazy world, we only had each other. I used to feel like I had Brian's protection at these parties, but that was over. Bill kind of took Brian's spot, but he was a hard man to understand. He could be kind and loving or pissed off and very controlling. With Brian, I had been able to let my guard down, but with Bill I never had that complete trust.

Everyone started leaving, and I was staying the night at Bill's. I asked if Tyler was coming and home and found out he wasn't. Bill told me to ask Troy if he wanted to stay, and he was able to. It was always nice hanging out with Troy and just being a regular kid for a while.

The first day of Christmas break, Brian asked if I could come over. I was pretty excited about it, but I didn't want him to know that. I replied, "I don't know. I have to ask."

"Who are you going to ask, Timmy?"

"My parents and Bill"

"I already asked Bill, and he said yes. Carlos is going to be here. I will pick you up in an hour at Thrifty's. I had been home more than usual the last week and had been on the receiving end of Mom's anger because of it. She was glad to get rid of me and said yes quickly.

By the time I got ready and walked to the store, they were waiting for me. It was Brian and Roger, Carlos and Joey. I said hello to everyone, even though it made me mad to have to be anywhere near Joey. He recognized me from school and his voice sounded kind of excited and he asked, "Hi, Timmy, do you remember me?"

"Yeah," I forced myself to sound friendly. I wanted to blame him for everything, but I knew it wasn't his fault. He was a victim, just like I used to be. He looked so young and small, like I was in the beginning. He had dark hair and naturally tanned skin. He was good-looking; he met all the criteria for the group. The sad part was the men would fall in love with him, and it would send his world spinning into utter darkness before he knew it.

I got in the car, and Joey moved to the middle of the seat. He was excited and started talking fast. He'd ask a question, and before I could answer, he had moved onto another subject. Brian and Roger started laughing.

"What's so funny?" I asked Carlos.

"Joey never talks; we don't know what got into him."

"How do you turn him off?" I asked Carlos. He just shrugged. "It's never been a problem before."

Roger turned around and said, "Joey, calm down."

Brian asked, "Is anyone hungry?"

"I'm starving," Joey yelled.

Everyone starts to laugh again, and I was confused one more time.

Carlos looked at me and answered the look on my face, "He's never hungry."

Brian took us to Bob's Big Boy Restaurant. Joey calmed down long enough to have a two-way conversation with me. We all had a great time at the restaurant, and I enjoyed being with these guys again. Brian drove to his house after we ate. Joey ran through the door after Brian opened it and said excitedly to me, "Come see my room!" Then he ran to open the bedroom door.

I ran after him, ready to set him straight. Roger saw what was going to happen and grabbed the back of my shirt and jerked me to a stop. He told me, "Don't tell him that used to be your room."

I reluctantly agreed, and he let me go.

Joey was showing me all my own stuff. He had no idea what a price all this had cost me. He had no idea what lay ahead in his own future. I let him brag about all this cool stuff and turn on the stereo. He wanted to play with the racetrack that Brian had bought me just last Christmas. I hammered him in a race, and he told me I was pretty good at this. I smiled and kept my mouth shut.

Carlos came in and said, "Timmy, let me take your place. Brian wants to talk to you."

I handed over the controllers and went looking for Brian. I found him in his bedroom. Brian and Roger were kicking back on the bed talking. I saw this as a great opportunity to wrestle with Brian. I got a head start so I could get enough height, and I landed on Brian's chest. It felt like the old days. Roger moved out of the way so he wouldn't have to be involved. Brian let me pin him and acted like I was so strong I was hurting him, but I knew better.

Brian said, "Okay, you win. Now get off me."

"Not until you say uncle!" I demanded.

"Uncle, huh?" He laughed and flipped me over and sat on me. "Now I won't let you up until you say uncle"

"Never!" I was having too much fun"

He started tickling me, and I had to give up then.

After we got done laughing, Brian got serious and turned to me. "I need you to do something for me," he said.

"What?" I asked, interested but nervous at the same time.

"I need you to break in the new kid."

"How am I supposed to do that?"

"The same way you did Troy."

I did not want to do this. I should have known there was a reason behind me being invited today. It wasn't just because Brian missed me and wanted to spend time with me. Those days were long gone. When was I ever going to wise up to that?

"Why doesn't Carlos do it?"

"He tried, but Joey freaked out."

No joke, any sane kid should freak out. I didn't want any part of this. I turned and started to walk out the bedroom door.

"Timmy, you are going to do this one way or another," Roger said. "You can do it the easy way or the hard way. It's up to you."

61

I didn't even acknowledge that I heard him. I just walked back to my old bedroom to find Carlos. I knew I needed his advice on this.

"Carlos, can I talk to you?"

He followed me out to the living room.

I was shocked and it showed in my tone of voice, "Do you know what they want me to do?"

"Yeah"

"And you are all right with this?"

"Yeah, I did it to you didn't I?"

"That was different."

"How"

"I don't know; it just was."

"Look, Timmy, better he learns it from you than someone he doesn't like. He's going to be in the group whether you like it or not. He needs to learn the ropes, and who better to teach him than you?"

"No way, Carlos"

"Hey, I tried. It has to be you."

"I just . . ."

"You just what"

"I just hoped . . . Brian wanted me back."

"I know, Timmy."

I walked back into the bedroom, and Joey was still playing with the race cars. He had both controllers in his hand and was talking like a newscaster.

"Joey, stop for a minute." I sat down on the bed, and he walked over to me.

"Yeah, what's up?"

"Do you know why I am here?"

"Yeah"

"You do?"

"Yeah"

"Okay, why do you think I am here?"

"To break me in"

"Do you know what that means?"

"Kind of"

"And you are all right with that?"

"No. But what choice do I have?"

I shook my head and said, "None."

"Will we have to do this in front of people?"

"Yeah, I think so."

"I don't want people watching me."

"I know, but it will be all right. I promise I won't hurt you."

"I know, Timmy. I also know this used to be your room and you used to be Brian's boy."

"How do you know?"

"I saw pictures of you and Brian together, and at school, I am sitting where you used to sit. Sometimes Brian even calls me Timmy. I just put it all together."

"Well, Joey, if you're ready, let's go put on a show."

We walked into the living room, and Brian, Roger, and Carlos were talking. They stopped talking, and I looked at them and said, "We're ready."

"Yeah, we're ready," Joey repeated.

All three of them were extremely surprised at Joey's attitude. Joey didn't have to do anything he hadn't already experienced. But it was the first time with someone other than Brian and the first time in front of others.

Afterward we went to the backyard, and I noticed Brian had added a Jacuzzi and a new barbecue. I figured he just had to catch up to all the other guys. Joey and I headed for the Jacuzzi, and everyone joined us a few minutes later. Joey was talking ninety miles a minute, and I jokingly said, "Well at least that didn't devastate him. "Everyone laughed.

I watched Brian's expression as Joey was talking. He had such a look of pride and love on his face. "I remember that's how he used to look at me" Carlos read the situation correctly and leaned over and whispered in my ear, "Timmy, it'll be all right."

"Yeah, but it will never be the same."

We stayed there and talked quite a while until we were all getting hungry again. We went to Joey's room to put on some clothes. I looked around for the clothes I had left there and couldn't find any.

I asked Carlos, "Where are my clothes?"

Joey answered before Carlos could, "They're out in the garage."

I went out there and found three boxes with my name on it. It made me sad to see my stuff boxed up and put away. The first one I looked in had my personal stuff, a lot of pictures of me and Brian, and even notes I had written to him. The second one had more pictures, but these were of me nude. It embarrassed me to see them. I knew there were times Brian took my picture, but I didn't know how often it had really been. Some were when I first met Brian, and I could see how young I looked then. The third box held my clothes, and I picked something to wear.

Brian came in and asked, "Did you find your clothes?"

"Yeah," I grabbed them and walked past Brian. I was fighting so many feelings that it was hard to talk. I hated the fact that he could just box up what we had and put it out of sight and out of his mind. I hated that he could replace me, and I knew I could never replace him in my life. I hated that he could love and care for another boy and yet the whole time was telling me how special and unique I was to him.

"Are you all right?" he asked, concerned about me. But I knew he couldn't change or fix our situation. I just walked out without talking. I didn't want to give away any more of my heart or feelings.

We left the house to go eat at a restaurant. It was nice, but not nearly as fancy as the one Bill had taken us to. I wanted to hate Joey, but at the same time, I found it hard to be mad at him. I knew he was the innocent in this whole picture. Joey was still talking so fast that it was hard to even answer him back.

I turned to Carlos and asked, "Does this kid ever shut up?"

Carlos laughed and said sincerely, "I'm telling you, Timmy, he never talked like this before. It's just with you that he acts like this."

I chuckled because I was finding it hard to believe him, and I told him so.

Carlos added, "Brian was really thrilled that you got Joey to come out of his shell."

I just shrugged my shoulders.

After dinner was over, we all went to a drive-in. Joey fell asleep about halfway through the movie, and we got to watch the last half in peace and quiet. When we got back to the house, Brian carried Joey up to his room and laid him down on the bed. Roger and Carlos were loading the car with their stuff and getting ready to go home. Roger and Brian were discussing something, but I couldn't quite hear what it was.

Finally Roger said to me, "Get your stuff, and I'll take you home."

"You can't do that! I can't walk in the door this late" If you guys want to get rid of me, then take me to Bill's house."

Roger agreed and dropped me off at the gate so I could get in. I went in the back door that they kept unlocked and left a note in the kitchen that I was staying in one of the guest bedrooms. I slept hard, and it was 11:00 a.m. the next morning before I woke up. I checked Tyler's room, and he wasn't home. I didn't feel comfortable knocking on Bill's bedroom door, so I headed for my storage room to get more clothes. Since there was a shower down there, I figured I would use it. But as I passed the Jacuzzi I decided that would feel even better.

I had a stupidly bright idea to add some dish soap and bubbles to the Jacuzzi. I didn't know how much to put in with so much water so I used a large amount. At first it was great but very soon I realized I couldn't control all the bubbles. It started overflowing and headed for the door. I looked for a way to shut off the Jacuzzi but couldn't find any. I opened the door that led outside to give a pathway for this mess. I knew Bill was going to kill me. Why had I ever thought this was a good idea?

I ran to Bill's room, hating the idea of waking him up with such a problem. I knocked on the door and heard, "It better be important, or you're dead!"

"Bill, it's me, Timmy."

"Come in." He was still lying in bed, and there was a woman with him.

I apologized for disturbing them, and the lady asked, "Is this your son?'

"No," Bill explained, "it's my son's friend."

I told him what I had done and how the bubbles were everywhere.

He just laughed and said, "Don't worry, Timmy. Tyler did the same thing." Then he told me where the shutoff valve was. I ran down to shut it off. The bubbles had completely filled the room. After I shut it off, I went back to tell Bill how bad it really was. He told me where Anna's phone number was, instructing me to call her and she would fix it.

I called her, apologizing and begging for her help all at once. She said she would be there in about an hour, and I thanked her profusely. It took a couple of hours to clean up the bubbles and water, and I was still thanking her when we were done.

Anna said, "Don't worry. I'll charge Bill for overtime. The extra money helps me out."

"Anna, I don't want you to charge Bill. I can pay you."

"Sure, Timmy, and where would you get that kind of money?"

She followed me to my storage room, and I took out the envelope. There was a lot more than there had been the last time I had been there. I realized that Bill had a key to my lock box and he had collected my money from Brian and Roger.

Anna's eyes kind of popped open when she saw all those hundred-dollar bills. "I was only kidding, Timmy. Bill pays me really well. I can't take any money from you."

"Well, how about a tip then?"

"No, Timmy, it's okay." She leaned down and kissed me on my forehead. "I have to run now. I'll see you later."

When I went back to the kitchen, Bill and his girlfriend were up and getting something to eat. I was afraid I was in trouble, but Bill showed no sign of being mad. He took me home later that day.

GIFTS

I spent most of Christmas break at Bill's house. I stayed home enough so Mom could see me, but not enough so she could find me and beat me. Now that my situation had changed, more of the men were asking to spend time with me. They always had to go through Bill though. I didn't feel forced to go with them, but in reality, I knew I probably didn't have a choice.

One day, a guy named Steve came over to Bill's to pick me up. He was tall and had brown hair and blue eyes and dressed really nice. He had been to most of the parties, but he was the kind of guy that didn't really stand out. He was quiet and laid back and wasn't one of the major players. Steve asked me if I wanted to go to Knott's Berry Farm. I jumped on that offer.

That day, I got my first ride in a Maserati. I could sense Steve's excitement in his voice and actions. It was obvious he wasn't used to kids. I think he read a book the night before. He asked questions about school and friends, and I told him stories that were funny. Then he asked about my family, and I got real quiet. He realized this was a mistake and quickly recovered asking me what my favorite thing to do was.

When he ran out of questions, I asked him some. I know most men find it really easy to talk about them. I asked him what he did for a living, and I learned he was a chemical engineer. Since I knew nothing about that, he talked the rest of the way, explaining things I could never understand.

When I spotted the sign for the park, he could see my excitement and asked, "Timmy, what do you want to do first?"

"The Corkscrew roller coaster" "The coaster was in the middle of the park, and we went right to it and waited our turn to get on. The ride attendant told Steve I was too small to ride. When I measured myself up next to the line, we found out he was right. I was disappointed, but Steve made the day a lot of fun, and I went on all the rides I could and played at the arcade. By evening, I could see that Steve was getting anxious to leave and knew what was on his mind.

We left the park, and I figured we were heading back to his house. But he pulled off the freeway a few exits down and turned into the driveway of a cheap motel. I waited in the car, realizing I had never had this happen before. But I also knew I was getting used to playing the game with the men in the group. Steve opened up the door, and his excitement at having me alone pushed him over the edge before he wanted to. As we kicked back on the bed I could smell the sweat from the day on him, and I asked if I could take a shower. Most of the men used this time for much more than just a shower. I figured he was the same, and this would give him a good time. I got in the shower and realized he wasn't coming in. I got out and asked him to join me and he finally got my meaning. We left a little while after that, and I could tell by the look on his face that he did have a good time.

He asked where to drop me off at. I told him to take me home. I pointed to where my house was and expected him to pull down a little farther and let me out. To my horror, he pulled into our driveway and I ducked down real fast. I yelled, "You can't drop me off at my house."

"Why?" Steve asked confused.

"I don't want to have to explain you to my parents."

"Oh, sorry" I could tell I needed to train this guy.

"Thanks, Steve, for taking me to Knott's Berry Farm. I had a great time."

"Timmy, I had a really good time too." He pulled out his wallet and handed me two hundred dollars and asked, "is that enough?'

"Yeah," I smiled.

"Would you tell Bill that I took good care of you?"

"Sure." I opened the door to get out.

"Timmy?"

"Yeah"

"Can I see you again?"

"Sure."

I walked to my door and listened like I always did. Things at home were going downhill fast. Mom and Dad were drinking and fighting. Dad would go to a friend's house and drink instead of coming right home. Mom was drinking at home and always complaining of a headache. It was more confusing than ever at home. Mom's moods changed quicker than usual. You could pass her in the hall and she would tell you she loved you. An hour later, you could pass her again and get slapped upside the head.

Tonight, I got in my room without seeing or bothering anyone. I put my stuff away and went to my brother's room and knocked on his door.

"Tommy, can I come in?"

"Yeah "Where have you been"

"Just out Why"

"Your stupid friend, Tyler, kept calling."

"Thanks, I'll call him back."

I went to the kitchen and called Tyler. "Hey, Tyler, what's up?"

"Dad thought Steve would bring you back here, and he was worried about you."

Bill took the phone from Tyler and asked, "Are you okay?"

"Yes, I'm fine."

"He didn't hurt you, did he?"

"No, sir"

"Good. We are going out of town for a few days to go skiing. The house is open to you. Anna will be staying here, so if you need anything just ask her. Okay?"

"Yes sir. Thanks."

I must have sounded disappointed because Bill asked, "What's wrong."

"Nothing" I hope you guys have a good time."

"Timmy, everything will be all right. Use the house. Hang out here and have fun. Don't forget Tyler's party on the twenty-eighth. We'll have a great time. Our party is on the first Saturday of the month instead of the last because of New Year's." Then he hung up.

I went back to my room, turned on the radio, and fell asleep.

The next day, I stayed at home, and Mom was in a good mood. Mom's family was coming over tomorrow for Christmas dinner. When they got together, anything could happen. At the last party, Mom's two sisters had gotten into a catfight. It was scary but entertaining all the same.

On Christmas Eve, we got to open one gift. Tommy got a cool train set, so large it took four of dad's friends to put it in the garage. It was amazing. The set was landscaped and had tunnels and lighted buildings. It was very cool. I didn't have anything that large, so I opened one of my boxes. It was a G.I. Joe doll. I was very disappointed but tried not to show it.

The next morning, we finished opening the rest of the gifts. I wish I could tell you that things turned around for me, but not this Christmas. My brother scored with a lot of electronic gifts. And I got all the accessories for the G.I. Joe doll. I was hurt because my mom and dad were not interested in making me happy or knowing what I liked. It didn't matter that I had a storage room full of cool gifts and more cash on hand than most adults. It was the feeling that they didn't really care about me. I tried to hide my true feelings, but my enthusiasm wasn't good enough for Mom.

Dad and Tommy went to the garage to play with the new train set. This was Mom's opportunity to deal with my ungratefulness. She grabbed the back of my hair, dragging me to my room yelling, "You ungrateful little bastard!" As we moved, she made sure my head kept hitting the walls and even the closet door. She opened my door and shoved me through then shut the door behind her. I was relieved that on this particular rampage had ended so soon.

To my horror, she returned fifteen to twenty minutes later with a new wire hanger. Of all my experiences with her rage, nothing compared to the damage and pain that this weapon did to my body.

She had promised to never use this again when she'd seen the blood and welts last time, but I guess she forgot that promise. She walked in yelling and screaming, and I completely panicked when I saw the wire. I tried to get around her to run out the door but she was big enough to block it with her body. The first hit went across my face and I went down curling into a tight ball, praying for any form of a miracle today. She was so angry I thought this time she might even kill me.

I guess my prayer or my screams, reached Dad in the garage. He came to my bedroom. He screamed at the top of his voice, "That's enough, Linda."

She stormed from my room, still yelling whatever came to her mind.

Dad looked at me, yet it felt like he didn't really see me. "You shouldn't have been so ungrateful, Timmy. Now you have ruined Christmas for all of us. Just stay in your room unless you need to go the bathroom."

Couldn't he see the tears and the pain? Couldn't he see the blood soaking through my clothes? Couldn't he make her stop beating us kids? Would it be so hard to put his foot down and make her realize what she was really doing to us kids?

I knew from experience that I had to take my shirt off now or the blood would dry and stick to my skin. I crawled to the bed and lay on my side, wondering why my parents disliked me so much. I knew some kids had parents that would love, cuddle, and protect them. I just didn't know why I didn't deserve parents like that.

I heard the family come in, and the house filled with talking and laughter. A lot of people had gathered today—my grandparents, aunts and uncles, and cousins—yet none of them came to see me. I have no doubt my mom made up a great story to tell my relatives. I only wished even one of them could have guessed the truth. I did the only thing that could bring me peace on the Christmas holiday. I fell asleep and dreamed of being somewhere else.

I woke up about 9:30 p.m. and moved slowly and carefully because of the pain. I inched my way down the hallway, not hearing any sounds at all. A careful check of the house, and I found I was all alone. Now that was a true gift to me. I raided the refrigerator since I had only eaten breakfast early that day. I ate everything cold, not wanting to take the time to warm it up—not wanting to get caught if they came home. I went back to my room and realized it would be really hard to sleep now.

I went to my mom's cabinet in her bathroom. So much medicine lined the shelves, it looked like a pharmacy. I found a bottle of Valium and took a couple in case just one didn't work. I went back to my room and took it. It didn't take long before I could feel the drug start to take effect. I shut off my light and lay down, getting as comfortable as possible.

I heard the front door open, and Mom walked to my room, opened the door, and said, "You can get up now if you want to." Her voice sounded like nothing was wrong.

I slept until about noon the next day. No one was in the house again, and I had nowhere else to go. I knew I couldn't ride my bike to Bill's house until I felt better, so I took another pill and went back to sleep.

Finally, I made it to December 28, Tyler party". It was going to be a great day, hanging out with Bill and helping get ready for the party. Bill picked me up early that morning. Since Dad was doing side jobs for him to make extra money Bill could really come get me anytime he wanted to. That was good news for me.

I knew what Tyler was getting for his birthday, and it wasn't the Porsche in his dad's garage that he wanted. No, Bill wasn't having his son drive a used car. Tyler was getting a brand-new, red Porsche 944 with a fin on the back of it.

Bill asked me if I wanted to go with him to pick it up. I was thrilled to be hanging out with him and excited to be a part of what was happening. He made me promise not to tell Tyler, but he already knew I was good at keeping secrets. Anna was in the car so she could drop us off at the dealership and do the paperwork. I was excited to ride in it before Tyler, and Bill was anxious to get behind the wheel and see how it drove. When we left the dealership, he squealed the tires and smiled proudly.

We got on the highway, and he looked around for cops then floored it. My head hit the back of the seat, and I saw the speedometer go past 100 mph. My heart was racing, and I was a little scared. Then Bill nodded his head in approval. He let off the gas and drove his normal speed.

"Well, Timmy, what do you think?"

"That was great!"

"Don't you ever tell Tyler how fast I drove, because if he does it, I will kill him."

I just smiled back at him.

"What should I get Tyler for his birthday?"

"How much money do you want to spend?"

"I don't know."

"Well, take a guess."

"I don't know." Whatever it takes to get him a good gift" I have a lot of money saved."

"I bet you do. How much do you have?"

"I don't know. I haven't counted it."

"Why?"

"I just haven't. I know I have two hundred that Steve gave me the other day. And I have the money in my room in the mattress, plus the money at your house."

"Are you crazy" What if your mother finds it?"

"She won't."

"We can't take that chance. Tomorrow you get that money from your mattress and put it in the storage room at my house. Do you understand me?"

"Yes, sir"

"Well do you want to impress Tyler?"

\ "Yeah"

"Then we'll say that you paid for the fin on his car."

"How much did it cost?"

"You don't want to know."

"We'll just say you bought it, and you can keep your money."

"I want to pay something on it."

"I'll tell you what. You give me the money you have in your pocket, and we'll call it even."

"It's only about fifty dollars."

"That will be plenty." He smiled down at me.

We drove through the gate and parked the Porsche behind the garage. Tyler would be at a friend's house until tonight, so he wouldn't see it. Bill finished by having the car wrapped in a huge yellow ribbon with a bow on top and a card that read, "Happy Birthday, Tyler."

I asked Bill, "Are we setting up for the party?"

"No, it's all being taken care of."

"What are we going to do?"

He gave me a look and raised his eyebrows. I could tell Bill was happy that he had two boys—one he could buy a car for and one he got his own personal pleasure from.

We walked into the house, and I figured we would go to the Jacuzzi and steam room. He passed the doors, and I realized he was heading toward the torture room with the racks in it. I stopped dead in my tracks; my brain was telling me to get out fast.

Bill saw that I stopped walking and asked, "What's wrong?"

"I don't like that room."

"Nothing bad is going to happen to you. I'm not going to hurt you. It's all pretend. You like to play pretend, don't you?"

I shrugged my shoulders like I wasn't sure, but I wanted to yell, *hell no*.

He took my hand and led me to the door. He had several locks on this door, and it took a minute to open all of them. The room looked the same; all the equipment and lights and mirrors were just like last time. Bill took his clothes off and told me to do the same. I was nervous and hoping for an easy time today. Bill surprised me. He wanted his wrists hooked to the cable and to be lifted to his tiptoes. He told me to whip him, and I did this as gently as I could get away with, not wanting to make him mad and be on the receiving end of a bad beating. He kept telling me to do it harder, and I worked my strength up to where he wanted. All the while, he was getting extremely excited. He tells me to stop, and it didn't take long before he was completely finished. The guys always felt they needed to return the favor. I think it helped make them feel that what was happening was okay.

With that out of the way, we went to the pool to swim for a while. Bill asked me, "So, Timmy, why were you so ungrateful this Christmas?"

"My brother got this really cool train set that sits on plywood with buildings and lights and all this stuff. You wouldn't believe the time and money they put into it. Then he got a new stereo and some really nice clothes."

"I see this upsets you. What did you get?"

"I got a G.I. Joe doll and some accessories. It sucks! I can't tell anyone at school about it. You don't give a guy a doll in the fourth grade."

He laughed. "You're probably right."

"Bill, I don't think I ever played with dolls. Do you think my parents are wondering if there is something wrong with me?"

"What do you mean?"

"Who buys dolls for their son in fourth grade?"

"I know you're upset, Timmy."

"Bill, is Carlos gay?"

"Timmy, all I asked you is what you got for Christmas. Where the hell is all this coming from?"

"I don't know. Is he?"

Bill hesitated then said, "Yes, Carlos is gay."

"Am I?"

"Timmy, why are you asking?"

"Everyone at school was teasing my friend Denny and calling him gay, fag, queer—all kinds of other names too.

"Oh, I see."

"I don't know who I am. I don't know what to think. I'm scared." I was getting really upset talking about it.

"Timmy, calm down. Look, you're different. That's why everyone loves you. That's why you're the favorite."

"No. Joey is going to be. He's the youngest."

"You're wrong about that. He might be the youngest, but that will change. You're special. Do you realize how many of the men call me and ask for you?"

"No."

"Well they all do."

"Except for Brian"

"No, that's not true. I told him he couldn't see you without my permission anymore. I'm not going to let him keep screwing with you to train his new pet. That's why he hasn't called you."

That explained a lot to me. "So, am I gay?"

"No you're not" You act like a boy, and you talk like a boy. And you hate dolls. I think that makes you all boy. Do you understand me?"

"Yes"

"Don't think on such things; you're too young."

He made me feel better, but I didn't feel so young. I felt lost and disconnected in this world. I felt like no one could understand me because I didn't even understand myself. I felt like there were three parts to me. The first was an abused, unwanted kid at home. The second was a semi-cool and finally accepted kid at school. The third wasn't a victim anymore but a willing participant with these men. This lifestyle seemed more exciting than my life at home. The money, attention, and compliments seemed to attract me and take away from the pain of what it was really costing me.

We got out of the pool and took a shower. Bill kept staring at me and finally said, "You are really something. Brian was an idiot for letting you go. Now let's talk about the party. I don't want any funny business from you."

"I know, Bill. I wouldn't do that."

"Timmy, you are going to be the only kid there. The rest of them are teenagers. And I want you to keep your clothes on at all times."

"Even if I go swimming" I asked slyly.

"Don't be a smart-ass!"

"Bill, I've been to other parties. I know how to act. But what about Tyler's "surprise"

"His car" What about it"

"No, not his birthday surprise" Tyler has a surprise for me tonight. I'm pretty sure he has a girl for me."

"I don't like you guys sneaking around and doing your own thing "Sorry, Bill, don't be mad. I didn't know we were sneaking around."

"It's not your fault, Timmy. It's Tyler's. I'll have a talk with him."

Before I could get dressed, Bill walked to his closet and got out a present for me from Tyler. I opened it really fast because I knew it would be a good one. There was a pair of expensive blue jeans and a really cool shirt and name brand tennis shoes. "This is great!"

"Try them on and see if they fit."

I put them on, and everything fit perfectly. "How did he know my size?"

"You've got clothes here. He just checked the sizes."

I looked in the mirror, and I realized I kind of looked like a rich kid in these clothes. I knew I would be the poorest kid at this birthday party, but it didn't matter.

Tyler came home, and I heard him calling for his Dad. I ran out of the room and yelled, "Happy Birthday!"

Tyler said, "Those clothes look really good on you."

"Yeah, thanks, Tyler! I really like them."

"When did you get here?"

"Your dad picked me up this morning."

Tyler looked at me kind of strangely and then asked, "Do you know what I am getting for my birthday?"

"No," I replied convincingly.

Bill was at the top of the stairs and said, "Tyler, I need to talk to you." I'm glad he didn't add my name because of the tone of his voice.

There were people all over the bottom floor, the game room and out in the backyard decorating for the party. I went to the indoor pool so I would stay out of the way of the workers and to keep my clothes clean. I took off my shoes and socks and rolled up my pants, thinking I could sit on the diving board and put my feet in the pool.

I was surprised at how much space was left between my feet and the water. As I sat there thinking about the fun that lay ahead for the night, the board began to bend, just enough so my feet could get wet. I quickly turned around; a little scared that I might fall in. There stood Carlos.

"What are you doing here?" I asked.

"I'm here for Tyler's birthday party. Is that all right with you?" he asked jokingly.

"Yeah" I was just surprised, that's all."

"Bill sent me to find you. People are starting to show up."

I followed Carlos back to the dining room where all the food was already prepared and set up. I looked the group over, and they all seemed to be preppies, jocks, or cheerleaders. The girls were especially beautiful, as if they were handpicked. Some of the kids were eating and drinking. Since the bar was open, they had their choice of alcoholic beverages also. I walked around the group feeling invisible, but that didn't really bother me.

I passed Carlos talking to three gorgeous girls. I spotted Tyler and headed to where he was talking to a group. I was stopped by a big, athletic looking guy, who told me to go get him a beer. I decided to give it a try and asked the bartender for a beer. He gave me one without even batting an eye.

When I took the beer back to the guy, he said, "Thanks, kid. Aren't you Tyler's little brother?"

Before I could answer, Tyler who, had walked over, put his hand on my shoulder and said, "He's my little cousin."

"Cool," the kid replied.

I didn't know where to go or who to talk to so I just stood around while everyone talked and ate. I really didn't feel like I belonged, but I was still glad I had been invited. I made a plate of food and went and sat on the patio. I was the only out there for a while. Finally three girls came out. One was blond and two were brunette.

The blonde said, "Hi, kid." She was absolutely hot! She had long, blond hair and beautiful blue eyes. She asked, "Who are you?"

"I'm Tyler's cousin," I answered, voice cracking from being nervous.

"Really" You're really cute."

"I blushed bright red" The blond introduced the other two, but I sat there staring at all of them, not even hearing her voice.

"What is Tyler like?" I finally heard the blond ask me.

I shrugged my shoulders, not sure how to answer, not even sure what information she was looking for. They turned to each other and started talking about Tyler. His good looks were the topic of some of their conversation, but they spent more time talking about how much money his dad had.

Bill found me sitting outside. "It's time for Tyler's present," he said. "Come with me." Bill had already pulled the car into the huge garage.

We went to the dining room, and Bill called Tyler to the center of the room where he was standing. A man rolled out a cake with sixteen candles lit, and everyone sang "Happy Birthday." Tyler was smiling and loving the attention. He blew out the candles.

With the flourish that a rich man could afford on such an important day, Bill led everyone to the garage. Tyler knew he was getting a car and wanted to act surprised when he got the older, black Porsche that his dad had bought a while ago. He had no idea there was a brand-new, red one with his name on it. Bill had put a blindfold on Tyler just before they walked through the door. Bill walked him to the front of the red car and asked, "Are you ready?"

"Yeah," Tyler replied.

Bill took off the blindfold and Tyler's face lit up. He was shocked to see the brand-new, red Porsche 944. He yelled really loud and turned to his dad and kissed and hugged him. He didn't seem to care who was watching. I thought that was cool. Then Bill and Tyler got in and went for a drive.

I went to find Carlos, and he was surrounded by girls still. I asked him, "Are you going to go swimming?"

A blond next to Carlos said, "That sounds like a great idea!"

I went to my storage room and changed into my swimsuit. By the time I got back, the girls were topless and wearing only their underwear and Carlos didn't have anything on. Even though I was overdressed I stayed that way and jumped in the pool. The girls were all over Carlos, flirting, teasing, and laughing, so I swam a little and then just sat on the steps and watched them for a while.

Finally some other teens came out of the house and joined the group. When Tyler came home, he jumped in the pool with all his clothes on, and the other kids just laughed. Bill saw me sitting there watching the whole thing. By now drugs were out in the open, and kids were drinking and pairing up to go have sex. He leaned down and said, "Come with me."

I got out and was shivering because the water had been so warm. I grabbed a towel and followed him far enough away where I could hear him over the music. He said, "I'm leaving now, and I want you to come with me."

"What about my surprise?"

"That isn't happening

So I got dressed, and Bill and I headed for his car. I was disappointed at having to leave early and pissed off that I wasn't going to get my surprise. You would think after all the sex these guys demanded from us that one time with a girl would be allowed.

I was quiet in the car and Bill asked me, "Are you upset?"

"Yes"

"Well get over it!"

"Yes sir" I knew not to push it with Bill. "Where are we going?"

"To Rick and Todd's house" He could tell I was disappointed and added; "Richard and Troy will be there."

I liked hanging out with Troy, but I was nervous anytime I had to go to Rick and Todd's house.

Troy saw me right after I walked in and said, "I didn't expect to see you here."

This statement made me think he had to spend a lot of time over at this house. I felt sorry for him because there was no telling what these guys were putting him through.

Bill went with the guys, and I followed Troy into the living room.

"Well since you're here, there's no telling what these guys have planned."

"No shit," I replied. This was not what I had planned for this weekend. It seemed I was always coming up on the short end of things. "How often are you over here Troy?"

"Too much

Then Bill and Rick walked over to us and started to explain what our roles would be for the movie they wanted to shoot tonight. Bill looked excited, and I realized that he probably had never been there when the movies were being made. I knew he had watched them.

The plot tonight was us two kids playing pool. I was the younger, inexperienced one, and Troy the older, more experienced player. For every ball I got in a pocket, he had to take something off, and the same went for me if he got a shot in. We played until we had no more pieces of clothing.

Then they turned the camera on, and Rick took Troy to one side of the pool table and Richard took me to the other. They both did it in such a way that it was painful. Troy and I were facing each other, and he reached out for my hand. It was comforting. When Todd turned off the camera, he told us he really liked the extra touch. He had no idea we really were reaching out for each other to find sanity in an insane world.

Our night was not over yet even though the camera was staying off. Todd and Bill were not going to be left hanging. When we were finished, Troy and I headed for the Jacuzzi to hang out and talk. I always wished afterward that the water could clean out the inside of me as well as it did the outside.

Troy asked me, "What happened to you and Brian?"

I explained it to him as best I could. It was hard because I was still confused about a lot of it. Then I finished with, "And Brian has a new pet, Joey."

Troy laughed and asked, "Why do you call him Brian's pet?"

"That's what Bill calls him."

We both laughed.

"I've met Joey before."

"How" I asked, curious because Troy and Joey didn't go to the same school.

"Brian had me come over to make friends with him. He wanted me to help break him in."

"How did that go?"

"Not so good. He doesn't trust anyone—especially not Carlos. He trusts you and Brian though. Otherwise, all he does is cry a lot. Since Brian isn't able to get you over to his house, I don't know if Joey will make it or not. Brian's going to talk to Bill and see if he can bring him over to his house and let you two hang out."

Hearing it put that way, I knew Brian hadn't just dropped me cold again. I knew Bill had put a stop to our communication or any arrangement that involved me and Brian seeing each other. It was easier for me to handle some of the pain knowing that.

The guys finally decided they wanted in the Jacuzzi too, and so Troy and I stopped our conversation altogether. The men were talking about how to keep improving on what they were doing. They were talking about better equipment and what it would cost. It sounded like Rick and Todd had found a market for selling and was explaining those details to the others. Bill was seeing the potential and asking a lot of business questions. Bill found out they had filmed about twenty movies already. But they were not of a good quality, and each of them would have to be redone to be sold on the market.

Hearing all this at once, Troy and I suddenly realized this could be sold to the public for the first time that the movies were going to be seen by others outside the group. And that we had an awful feeling. We weren't proud of what we were doing. We were caught in a world we didn't know how to get out of.

I had heard enough bad news for one night, so I got out and Troy followed me. I went back to the house to dry off and get dressed.

Troy asked sarcastically, "Timmy, how many movies did you do?"

"I don't know!"

"You don't know how many you've done?!"

"No! I don't! Do you know how many you've been in?"

"Yes, seven or eight, and you were in all of them."

"Troy, I do my best to forget things like this."

"How many do you think you've been in?"

"I don't know, maybe around twenty."

"You're in all twenty!" Troy yelled.

"Probably" I'm not sure! If I had a choice I wouldn't have been in any of them! Don't you get it? "Who was with you in the other ones?"

"I don't know. Nick and Carlos, you, and I guess the guys."

"What guys?"

"You know, Rick and Todd. They would wear masks; sometimes there was a third guy too."

"Who was that?"

"I think it was Richard."

"No shit!" Troy said, shocked.

"It was before you were in the group."

"I know. Richard had said he was in a couple movies, but I didn't believe him."

"What difference does it make?"

"None" I guess. I'm hungry."

I yelled outside, "Rick, we're hungry."

"Help yourself" he yelled back.

By the time I turned around, Troy had the refrigerator open, and he made himself a sandwich. I took an apple just to tide me over until the guys cooked. I saw the steaks marinating in the refrigerator, and I was waiting for the good stuff.

I was nervous after hearing the guys' conversation. I was used to Rick and Todd and Richard getting all excited about the movies. But when Bill joined in, I felt like I had lost a safety barrier or a protector from the worst evil we had to experience. If Bill went to their side, who would watch out for me? I knew the guys were excited about sucking Bill into this movie deal. He was a very rich man and an extremely influential one.

Troy and I sat silently while the guys continued making plans.

To my surprise, Rick said, "I would like to get Joey for a few movies."

We all turned to stare at Bill to see what his reaction would be.

Then Todd interjected, "Brian would never give him up."

"We got Timmy from him, didn't we?" Rick said.

The next thing I knew they were all staring at me.

"I can get him. I can get Brian on board. He called me the other day, asking if he could borrow Timmy," Bill said.

I couldn't believe what I was hearing! They were taking about us like we were items to be lent out, not real people.

"He thinks that, without Timmy, we are going to lose Joey," Bill said. "Timmy is the only one he trusts."

Rick asked, "What did you tell him?"

"That I would think about it," answered Bill.

Todd asked Bill, "Is Joey going to be at the party on Saturday?"

"No. He's not ready according to Brian. I'll set up a time for Timmy and Joey to get together. Then I'll know if he's ready or not."

Todd got up to turn the steaks over, and this was our chance to get up and leave the table also. We went to the living room to watch TV.

Troy turned to me. "Timmy, I don't have a good feeling about this."

"Me neither," I answered. But I knew we were both powerless to change anything these guys put into motion.

We fell asleep, and Bill had to wake me up to leave. It was 2:00 am, and I fell back to sleep in the car on the way home.

I was shocked at how bad the house looked when we walked in. Beer cans and trash were all over the place. People were passed out, some with their clothes on and some without. Bill told me to go to one of the guest rooms and go to bed. There were four of them, but they were all full of teens. For the most part, each boy had a couple of girls next to him.

The last place I checked was Tyler's room, and he wasn't sleeping alone either. Bill happened to walk up behind me, and I told him the guest rooms were all full. He took me to his room, and I was asleep by the time my head hit the pillow. I didn't wake up until after 11:00 am the next morning. I was still dressed in my clothes, and I got out of bed quietly, not waking Bill up.

I could hear a lot of voices and looked and saw it was the cleaning crew. All the kids were gone by now, so I went to Tyler's room and found that he was alone and sleeping soundly. I went downstairs and saw Anna. "Boy, were you at the party last night?" she asked.

"No, ma'am"

"Good. Because when I got here this morning it looked like Sodom and Gomorrah, boys and girls everywhere. So she turned to face me, if you weren't at the party" I saw her early and had to leave the party early, when did you get here?"

"I came in about 2:00 am "I was with bill."

She looked at me puzzled.

"I was out with Bill."

She looked away, disgusted. Then she asked, "Are you hungry, boy?"

"I'm starved." I had only had an apple before I fell asleep last night.

"Good! Let me cook you some breakfast."

We made small talk, but I knew she really wanted to ask me about the time she saw me and Bill. It was hard for her to find a way to bring it up.

Anna turned around and asked, "Timmy, why are you here?"

I smiled, knowing what she really meant but jokingly answered, "Waiting for breakfast."

She turned back to the stove, and Bill came up behind me saying, "Hey, what's going on?"

I answered, "Anna is making me breakfast."

"Oh she is, is she?"

"Yes," Anna answered. "Would you like something to eat?"

"Yes," Bill answered. "What were you guys talking about?"

I cleverly answered, "We were talking about Tyler's new car."

I heard Anna cough a little and then she added, "That is quite some gift." Then she put a plate down in front of me with eggs, bacon, hash browns, and biscuits.

Bill and Anna kept talking while I ate like a starving boy. Tyler and Carlos came walking in together. Carlos patted me on the head. Tyler gave me a hug and thanked me for his birthday present. He walked over to Anna and gave her a big hug, lifting her off the ground and thanking her also. Now she had everyone to cook for, but this didn't faze her a bit.

One of the men from the cleaning crew announced that they were finished and that the caterers were here to set up. I had forgotten that it was Saturday and they were setting up for our party.

Tyler asked, "Dad, can Timmy come with me to the beach house today?"

"No."

"What about Carlos?"

Carlos spoke up, "Roger is coming to pick me up."

Tyler was really disappointed. "Dad, why can't Timmy go? I'll take good care of him."

Bill answered, "Sorry, Tyler; his parents want him home."

Tyler was mad and grabbed his packed bags and headed for the door. Bill walked out after him. Carlos and I shrugged our shoulders. Anna was just watching everything unfold. A few minutes later, Bill came back in and motioned for Carlos and me to follow him. He took us to his office.

"Timmy, I talked to Brian this morning and he should be on his way over with Joey," Bill said. "We want you to spend some time with him before the party."

"Doing what?" I asked cautiously, even though I knew the answer.

"Play games with him in the game room; swim with him in the inside pool. See if you think he can make it through a party."

I nodded my head in agreement then asked, "Is Carlos going to help me?"

"No, it's better if we do it this way."

Then he handed me an envelope and said, "This is for last night. Now go put it in your room. And don't forget to get the money you have in your mattress at home. I want to know how much you have at all times and let me know when you take money home."

"Yes, sir"

I left Bill and Carlos talking and went straight to my room and checked my money, it was all there. I couldn't believe how much I had saved so far. I felt like I was rich! I walked back to the main part of the house and was surprised when I looked up and saw Brian and Joey walking toward me.

I tried to act nonchalant at seeing Brian, but a big smile still spread across my face. He gave me a hug and then I turned to greet Joey. He had a fake smile and had the saddest eyes.

Brian said, "I'll leave you two alone," and walked to Bill's office.

"Joey, what's wrong?"

He just looked at the floor and shrugged his shoulders.

"Let me show you around. This place is awesome. Let's go to the game room."

He lit up when he saw how huge this game room was. "Wow!"

"It's cool isn't it?"

"Very cool,

We played air hockey and I let him win a few. Then we bowled a few games, and I could tell he was finally starting to relax.

"Timmy?" Joey asked.

"What?"

"I'm worried about the party tonight"

"What are you worried about?"

"I don't want to go. I'm scared."

"I used to be scared too."

"You're not anymore?"

"No."

"Why?"

I still got nervous with every party. In time, you could get used to almost anything, no matter how sick and twisted it really was. But I couldn't say that to poor little joey.

"Look, Joey, you are with Brian, and he won't let anything happen to you." This was a line of bull! "You aren't afraid of Brian are you?"

He surprised me and answered, "Yes."

"Why?"

"Because he is always telling me how much he loves me, how beautiful I am, and the whole time he's doing things to me that I don't like."

"Why haven't you told your parents?"

"I live with my dad. I don't know where my mom is."

"Have you told your dad?"

"Yes."

"You have?!"

"Yeah, but we're poor. He knows Brian and we need the money."

"No shit!" I was surprised that he had his dad's permission. I was even more surprised that his dad didn't care what other men were doing to his son! He was selling Joey to Brian and the group for money. I had been where Joey was, I felt sorry for him. "Joey, do you trust me?"

"Yeah"

"Look at it like a game, and we are actors doing what we get paid to do. We make a lot of money. I can't protect you because I'm in the same situation as you. But we can stick together and help each other through it. You stay close to me, and I'll stay close to you. Okay?"

He didn't look convinced but said, "Okay."

We left the game room, and I showed him the gym and the inside pool and even my locker room. "Do you want to go in the Jacuzzi?"

"Yeah"

I had been in this house enough to know how to use the equipment. I had already turned down the heat on the Jacuzzi to where I liked it. I took off my clothes and got in the water, and he did the same. We sat and talked, and I learned a lot about him.

Troy walked in a while later, and Joey immediately started shutting down again. Troy got in the water, and Joey moved as far away as he could without being obvious.

"Joey, what's wrong?" I asked.

He shrugged his shoulders.

"Troy is all right. He's like me and you. We need him, and he needs us. We all have to stick together. The more of us there are, the easier it is on us. Do you understand, Joey?"

"I think so."

Then I put my arm around Joey and the other arm around Troy, and we talked some more.

Punishment

Carlos walked in. I could tell right away that he wasn't himself. He got in and sat across from us.

"Is everything all right?" I asked Carlos.

Troy and Joey stopped talking to listen to our conversation.

"Roger and Bill are really mad at me! Roger even threatened to send me home. Bill threatened to kill me."

"Why?"

"Because I was at Tyler's' party."

For the first time, I was glad I wasn't there. "What did you do?"

"What difference does it make?!"

"It can't be that bad."

"Yes, Timmy, it can" Then he got out of the water and said, "Timmy, Troy, I need to talk to you guys. Joey, will you excuse us?"

Joey nodded in agreement.

"It's time for the party to start. I think they may make me pay for my mistake tonight. You need to obey the guys and do whatever they tell you to do. I don't care what I have to do, as long as Roger doesn't send me back to Puerto Rico."

I knew what he meant because I had been on the receiving end of punishment during one of these parties.

It was time to go to the backyard and start entertaining. I knew Joey would be extra nervous, so I told them to follow me and we took a shortcut to the pool. We did something that we knew the guys would enjoy. We all held hands and started yelling and ran straight to the pool and jumped in. This took away any chance of Joey chickening out.

There were a lot of men already, and they laughed at the spectacle that we made. Once we got in the pool, some of the men joined us and we picked teams for volleyball. The men were intrigued with Joey, the new kid, but they had been told to go easy on him and that I would be watching over him tonight.

I felt bad for Carlos and Joey—Carlos because the night would be about him and that was never good with this group, Joey because it was going to be the worst night of his young life. He was entering a sick, dark world and would lose even more control over his future. I couldn't begin to understand having a dad that was willing to turn his kid over to this madness. I could only wonder what else Joey's dad was willing to put him through.

Brian got in the pool and came over to me. "Is everything all right with Joey?" he asked.

"Yeah" Is everything all right with Carlos?"

"No, it's not, and there's nothing you can do about it."

"Yeah, I know. I hate it for him."

He smiled back in an understanding way.

I got out of the pool and walked to the room that we were going to use tonight. It was already set up. I had been to enough of these that seeing the room gave me a good idea how and what these guys had planned. Plastic covered the floor, two racks stood in the center of the room, and two tie-downs hung from the rafters. Bill and Roger were leaning over a table writing down the series of events that were going to take place.

Bill looked up and snapped, "Timmy, you know you're not supposed to be in here right now"

"I know."

"Then get the hell out of here!"

"Can I please talk to you?"

Bill was mad but agreed. He walked up to me and put his hand on the back of my neck, leading me to his office. "What's so important that we have to talk right now?"

"I'm worried about Carlos."

"What! Did Carlos send you to talk to me?"

"No! He has no idea!"

Bill looked straight into my eyes with a noticeable threat and said; you just do what you're told and remember there are two racks out there! For all you know you could be right next to him!" He saw how scared I was and said, "Now get back to the party"

I turned around and ran right back to the party. We played four or five more volleyball games in the pool, and then the guy cooking yelled that the food was ready. Once again, we made our plates so we could eat after all the activities were over. The guys kind of ate in shifts, still keeping up a game of volleyball for us kids.

Carlos swam over to me and asked, "Where did you go earlier?"

"I went to talk to Bill."

"About me"

"You"

"You asshole" He pounded me hard in the chest, knocking the wind out of me. "Why can't you mind your own business?" Then he grabbed my hair and pushed me under the water. Steve, one of the men, came over and pushed Carlos off me. I came up gasping for air.

Steve yelled, "That's enough, Carlos!"

Carlos got out of the pool and sat in a chair and glared at me. Steve stood by me until I caught my breath again, and then I got out of the pool. I went straight to the closet with the cleaning supplies and got a broomstick. I walked back to the pool and up behind Carlos. He was sitting with his elbows on his knees and his head in his hands. I was so sick of him hitting me when he got mad that I wanted to get my revenge this time. I swung that broomstick as hard as I could and hit him across his shoulder blades. Some of the guys had yelled for me to stop but it was too late.

He screamed in pain and fell to the ground. I raised it back up for a second hit, and one of the men grabbed me and jerked the stick out of my hands.

It took no time for Bill and Roger to come outside. Carlos was crying, and I was standing there gloating about finally getting back at Carlos for all the beatings. My triumph didn't last long. I saw the look on Bill and Roger's face and knew I was in big trouble. Bill said sternly, "Go to my office now!"

I had so much going through my mind now that I had finely got Carlos back for all the times he beat me up! I was sick of it I finely stood up for myself. I knew I loved Carlos, but I had gotten totally fed up with him than it hit me wrong place wrong time to lose my temper. Bill came in the room and yelled, "Who the hell do you think you are?!"

I was crying, but I spoke clearly, "I'm your boy."

Bill looked surprised and then smiled at me.

I knew this was my cue to run up and hug him. I kept repeating, "I'm so sorry." Then I tried to explain what had led up to the incident, but I was probably hard to understand I was speaking so fast.

"It's all right, Timmy. Steve saw it all and explained it to me."

"I just got fed up. He's always picking on me when no one is looking."

"I thought Carlos was a good friend to you?"

"He is, most of the time. I just finally lost my temper."

"This can never happen again at one of the parties. Do you understand? Now the guys are all freaked out. We've never had two kids fighting."

"I'm really sorry, Bill. It will never happen again."

Roger and Carlos walked into the office. Carlos was still hurting bad. Roger led him to a chair and told him to sit. Carlos looked at me like he wanted to kill me.

"Carlos, I'm sorry."

"I'm sorry too," Carlos said, but the words never reached his eyes.

"This better never happen again!" Bill said. "Timmy, this night isn't just about Carlos anymore. Welcome to his world." Then Bill walked out the door.

Roger handed Carlos a couple of strong pain pills, and Carlos wasted no time swallowing them.

Carlos looks at me with great satisfaction and says, "Thanks for taking half the beating for me tonight. The only difference between us tonight is that you will feel the pain, and I won't." Then he walked out of the room.

I followed him and said, "You bastard!"

He turned and smiled smugly and said, "Yes I am. Thank you very much!"

"All you care about is yourself. I tried to help you tonight."

"And you've done a great job of it."

We walked into the great room, where all the men were gathered except Brian and Joey. I figured he had decided tonight was not a good night to start Joey. We both apologized sincerely to the men.

The men were ready for the activities to start. Troy was already buckled and chained. His feet barely touched the floor. Todd walked me to the rack, and Bill took Carlos to the other rack, and they tied us down. They turn the racks so we were facing each other. I could see that the pills had already started taking effect. I knew I was screwed.

I jumped when Todd hit me several times, even though it wasn't real hard. Bill was hitting Carlos hard enough that he could feel it even through the medicine. Carlos was not acting now. He was hurting, and he was breaking. These whips weren't the kind that landed easy either. We used those when we were making movies. These had some real sting to them.

Todd pulled my head back and asked, "Did you learn your lesson tonight?"

"Yes, sir"

Carlos was yelling so loud we both turned and watched. I cringed knowing what was coming next for me. I tried to keep count so I might have an idea how many I would have to endure. After about twelve to fifteen hits, Roger told Bill that was enough. Carlos was crying so hard that it scared me.

Todd reached down and unbuckled my arms and legs and said, "Tonight is your lucky night. No more fighting." Then he grabbed the back of my neck forcefully. He leaned down and said in my ear, "And don't ever try to leave the group again!"

I looked him in the eye and nodded, scared to death.

Roger helped Carlos out of the room, and I could see the sympathy on the men's faces. That was unusual because they usually got off on the severe beatings. I had been beaten, and it wasn't sympathy I saw on their faces.

Troy was also released, and he walked over to me and asked, "Now what?"

"I don't know."

Then to my surprise Brian walked in with Joey. That was what the men had been waiting for. They were just waiting for the other events to get over with. I could sense the change in their mood immediately.

Now they brought out the baby oil, and the night was finally coming the grand finale. It was uneventful for the most part, and Joey ended up doing well for having to endure a new level of participation.

Afterward, we got our plates of food and reheated them and ate heartily. Joey was still nervous, so I took him to a quiet place to eat. Troy followed us, and we ate in silence.

When we were done I told Joey, "You did good Joey I said the guys loved you. Don't be nervous; nothing else is going to happen tonight." At that point I believed joey was the whole reason they were easy on us today.

He looked at me so grateful for that news and the support that he reached over and hugged me. Troy and I laughed because we had been in his shoes too. I felt bad because I had helped introduce him into this dark, sadistic world. But I knew that circumstances beyond our control had brought all us kids to this point in our lives.

It was late, and the men started leaving. Soon enough it was only Bill and me left. We put away anything that pertained to the entertainment that night and left the food and drinks for the cleaning crew the next morning. Bill and I went to his room and showered, and I got in bed first. When Bill got comfortable, I got next to him and laid my head on his chest and said, "Thanks for not letting them beat the hell out of me."

He smiled and said, "You're welcome. I just didn't want to spend the night babying you."

I went home the next day, and Mom had already put up all the Christmas decorations. The house was empty, and I hung around for a while. Finally, I left a note and headed to Denny's house. I took some of my own money and bought some more candy to act like I was selling. Denny was happy to see me and showed off all he had gotten for Christmas. It was near dinner time, and I was invited to stay, but I knew I had to be home tonight because I had been gone so much. And didn't want mom to have a reason to be piss off at me!

I wasn't sure what kind of mood mom would be in. Dad was out of town doing jobs because money was so tight. Mom and Dad were fighting more than ever, and Mom was drinking a lot, even when dad was home. I think she felt like she was losing him and this kept her in a bad mood all the time. And when that happened she continued to vent her anger on us boys. I ended up going home.

I could hear my mother screaming at Tommy even before I got to the door. It sounded like she was tearing the house apart, but I knew by my brother's screams that it wasn't the house that was getting shredded to pieces.

I snuck in the house and went straight to my room and kept the light off. I was hoping Mom would forget all about me. I lay on my bed with my eyes closed and my hand over my ears. At times like this, I would wish, hope, pray, anything to make her disappear from our lives. I would even wish she was dead. I felt bad about that, but it was hard to believe that she really did love us when these beatings happened so often. I would picture Dad raising us by himself and there was no bad side to that. But if Mom and Dad split, I know he would leave us with Mom and that scared the hell out of me. I was angry with Dad too because he rarely made her stop.

When I was young, I just thought Dad really didn't know what was happening when he was gone. Or maybe he couldn't hear us screaming from the other end of the house. I'd grasp on anything to believe so that I could feel like one of my parents loved and protected us. But I was slapped with reality about a week ago.

Dad and Tommy were playing with the new train set in the garage. I just wanted to be around them, so I acted like I was cleaning my bike. I was shocked to hear Tommy say to Dad, "You know she's beating us." I couldn't believe Tommy was actually talking to Dad about this.

"Yeah" Then he shocked me with the rest of his answer. "It won't kill you. As long as she is beating you, she is leaving me the hell alone." Then he chuckled.

I stormed out of the garage, slamming the door as I left. But I still heard him say, "Better you than me." That son of a bitch knew and just didn't care.

That night after my parents went to bed, Tommy snuck in my room to tell me what else had been said. He started out, "Dad knew we were getting beat."

"I know. I heard."

"He thinks you get it worse than I do."

"What do you think?"

"I used to think so, but now you're gone a lot, and I think I do."

I nodded my head in agreement. From the way Tommy talked about Mom, I knew he hated her too.

"Where do you go all the time?"

I told him a little about Denny, Tyler, Troy, and Carlos, being really vague about what we did. He seemed a little jealous. He used to be the one with a bunch of friends, and now I finally had a lot too. He even told me that Dad was glad when I was gone and that Mom had no complaints either. I knew it to be the truth, but it was still hard to hear it. They never cared or even asked where I was going. When I did get home, they never asked about what I had been doing. As I got older, I wouldn't even get in trouble for coming in really late. Mom didn't really care, but if she wanted an excuse to beat you, she would say that you should have been home.

The men always made sure I was home at a decent time so my parents wouldn't get suspicious and start asking questions like normal parents would. But I knew the reason behind Dad wanting me to be gone. He knew Mom wouldn't be so upset and that I was really safer if I was gone. If only he knew that hadn't always been the case. Tommy left and went to bed. I lay there, contemplating my screwed up life.

My bedroom door flew open and hit the wall. The hall light shone right in my eyes so I couldn't see. But I knew who was standing in my doorway, and with an entrance like that, my mom wasn't there so she could kiss me good night.

She said, "Oh, there you are! "I don't remember the rest of it because my mind would freeze up at times like this. She began beating me and screaming. I rolled into a tight ball and couldn't help but cry from the pain. She was hitting me so hard that I tried to crawl on the floor to get away. Then she picked me up by my neck and slammed me into the dresser. I had developed such a deep fear of my mother that it could actually paralyze me. I couldn't think or talk, let alone speak. There was no right answer to any of her insane questions anyways. When her anger ran out, she left and made sure to slam my door.

I stayed on the floor, shivering from fear and cold, too afraid to move. She had really gotten me good in my stomach and chest tonight. My head and neck were screaming in pain from hitting the dresser. I grabbed my blankets and crawled under my bed, giving me the false security I needed to fall asleep.

"The I Don't Care Pill"

The next morning I could hardly move. My neck and back hurt really badly. I crawled out from under the bed and was shocked to see what time it was. It was already 10:00 a.m. I was really late for school. Tommy probably checked on me and thought I had left already. I dressed quietly and quickly, not daring to go to the bathroom and to wash and brush my teeth.

I listened at the door and could hear Mom on the phone in the kitchen. I knew the only way out now was through the garage. When I opened the garage door it squeaked a little; to me, it sounded extremely loud. Mom was too far away to hear it, and I got my bike and started to school. I knew showing up late could start questions that might be hard to answer, so I decided to ditch for the day. I hadn't had breakfast yet and was hungry. I went to a nearby doughnut shop and picked a couple of doughnuts and took a seat near the front window.

I noticed a man walking in who looked familiar, but I wasn't sure where I knew him from. He caught me looking at him and smiled and said, "Its Timmy right?"

Then I realized he was one of the guys from the group. He wasn't a major player, and I couldn't even begin to try to remember his name.

"Yeah," I answered hesitantly.

He sat down at my table and said, "Do you know who I am?"

I looked right at him but wasn't sure how to answer that. How did you tell someone that he looks different with his clothes on? "Do you remember my name?"

I shook my head no.

"Can't you talk?" he asked with a slight laugh.

I took a drink of my milk like it was whiskey giving an alcoholic some strength.

"Yes, I can speak. I was just caught off guard. And I couldn't remember your name." He looked like his feelings were a little hurt, so I added, "At least your real name. I think I've heard them call you Mark."

This brought a smile to his face, and he said, "Yes, that's right."

I caught him looking me over and figured he wanted to make plans with me or something. It made me feel nervous.

Instead I was surprised by his question. "Why do you look like someone beat the hell out of you? I saw you outside, and you walked like a stiff, old man. You have a bruise on your forehead and bruises all over your arms. And why aren't you in school today?"

Well, I give him credit for reading my body language. So I answered his question. "I woke up late. I had to sneak out of the house so my mom wouldn't hear me. I didn't want to go to school and have questions rose about all my bruises, and I was hungry, so I stopped here. I walk funny because I got an ass whooping last night." Apparently I said all this with a little too much attitude.

Mark asked, "Why are you mad at me?"

"I'm sorry. I'm just really hungry and in a lot of pain. I'm afraid of getting caught ditching school."

"Why did you get an ass whooping?"

"Could we please talk about something else?"

"Sure. Like what?"

"Like why you're here and not at work."

"Because I'm rich and don't have to work."

"Really"

"Yes, well kind of."

"What does that mean?"

"I am rich. I own a couple of businesses, and when I'm there, half the time I don't know what I am doing. So I hire people to run them, and every once in a while I show up and act like I know what I'm doing." Even though he downplayed his part I had the feeling he was very smart and knew exactly what he was doing. "So what are you going to do the rest of the day?"

"I have no idea."

"Why don't you hang out with me today?"

I knew what that usually meant from these guys so I said, "Just look at me!" I was in no shape to entertain anyone.

"Timmy, I'm not going to hurt you. Just hang out with me, and we will have some fun. I promise. Plus, I wouldn't want to piss Bill off."

I smiled and asked, "Are you as rich as Bill?"

He laughed out loud and said with much drama, "God's not even that rich!"

I finished eating and drinking and walked with him to his car. He had a two-door convertible. I asked, "What are we going to do with my bike?"

"Can you lock it up?" He could tell I was concerned, so he said, "Let me go talk to the manager. I know him."

He went and talked and I was wondering what I was getting myself into.

"Take your bike around to the back door, and they'll put it inside."

I walked around, and a small, Oriental man opened the door and said, "Hey, kid, put your bike in here. Are you all right?"

"Yeah," I answered, surprised by his question.

"So you know this man?"

"Yeah I do."

"Okay then."

I got into the car with Mark, and he asked, "What do you want to do today?"

"I don't know."

"You can do anything you want. Just tell me."

"I want to go to the beach, walk down the pier, and eat ice cream.'

"That we can do"

He turned the car around and headed for the freeway. I asked, "Do you have any kids?"

His voice was a little sad when he answered, "Yes, two girls. Their mother left three years ago and lives somewhere in Texas. I haven't seen them since."

I made a mental note to stay off this subject with him in the future. I said sincerely, "I'm sorry." I looked out the window, and we were both quiet for a little while.

Mark asked, "How is it being Bill's boy? Does he spoil you?"

"Yeah, he's really good to me."

"Do you stay at his house a lot?"

"Yeah"

"Don't your parents care?"

No, not really. Let's not talk about my family."

"Okay. Why do you like the beach so much?"

"I have a lot of good memories there."

"How's that"

"Brian used to take me there a lot."

"Oh, I see. Do you miss Brian?"

"A little"

"So, do you like Joey?"

"Yeah"

"Are you mad at him for taking your place?"

"At first I was."

We talked some more about each of the kids in the group. I found out Mark had been in the group for about four years.

We finally made it to the beach and parked and went out on the pier. The wind blew a lot on the pier, and it was getting cold. The ice cream shop was closed, and I was a little disappointed. Mark was surprised that I wasn't more upset. I wish those were the only kind of problems in my life. We sat down on a bench and watched the water for a long time without talking.

We got up and moved to a different place and saw some surfers. I said, "I bet those guys are freezing."

"No, the wet suits they're wearing are keeping them warm. Have you ever surfed before?"

"No."

"I used to before I got married. Maybe this summer I can teach you."

"Are you getting hungry?"

"Yeah, all I've had were those donuts."

We stopped at a great chicken place, and I ate a lot. We got back on the freeway to go home, and I realized he was getting off at a different exit. I got nervous because of past experiences.

He noticed and told me, "Don't worry I just want to stop by my house and show you the surfboards that I have. I'll show you the one that would be perfect for you to learn on."

His house stood far away from his neighbors, and a white, rail fence surrounded the property. The neatest thing I saw were some horses grazing.

"Are those your horses?"

"Yes, do you like to ride?"

"I've never ridden before."

"Maybe we can do it sometime."

"Really"

"When can you come over?"

"Tomorrow after school"

"Really" His voice sounded excited.

"Can you pick me up?"

"Sure."

We pulled into his driveway. The house was older but very nice. It was a Victorian style with pillars in front. Fifty acres surrounded the house. We walked over to the fence and looked at the horses. They were all different colors and were each very beautiful "You can ride any of them except the black horse," Mark said. The black horse was his, and he had a lot of spirit.

We walked back to the house, and he opened the garage door. I was extremely relieved to see surfboards hanging from the walls. He showed me a really fancy board that was his favorite to ride. I looked around, and a yellow and black one caught my eye.

"Do you like that one?" Mark asked.

"Yeah, it's cool"

"Good. That's the one I wanted to show you. If I teach you how to surf, that is the one you will be using."

"Wow!"

We went into the house, and it was very large and open. It had a classy country look to it. There were wood floors and antique furniture and landscape pictures on the wall.

"This house has been in my family for several generations."

"So your parents died and left it to you?"

"No. They retired and moved to Florida. They are very much alive," he laughed. "What time do you have to be at home?"

"Around 4:30." I knew I could stay longer but I didn't know him well enough to feel comfortable yet. And I still wasn't sure if he had anything else in mind. He seemed like a nice guy and had seemed honest enough so far, but I still knew what drew him to those parties.

We walked all around the house. Then he took me to the stables. The horses were big and beautiful. I found myself watching a white and brown painted horse.

Mark asked, "Do you like that one?"

"Yeah, he's beautiful."

"Well, he's a she, and her name is Crystal."

A solid brown horse came into view, and I asked, "Is it a boy or a girl?"

"You mean a male or female. That's a male, and his name is lightning."

"Can I ride him sometime?"

"Probably not him since you've never ridden before, Crystal is a good one to learn on. "One by one, he told me about each of the horses and their personalities.

It was finally time to leave, and Mark took me back to the doughnut shop where my bike was. He gave me his number and told me to call him, and we could hang out again. But he also asked me to keep it kind of a secret from Bill. I wasn't sure why since he hadn't hurt me or anything, but I still gave him my word. It seemed that each of these men in the group liked having secret lives.

The manager gave me my bike back, and I rode straight home, hoping today would be a better day. I heard laughter even before I opened the front door. Mom and Dad and Tommy were in the kitchen laughing and joking around. I realized it had been a long time since I'd heard a positive, happy sound in my house. Not wanting to interrupt their good time or accidentally put an end to it, I announced I was home and went to my room. I lay there listening to the radio and went over the day in my head.

It would be nice to ditch school tomorrow and just be a carefree kid, with learning how to ride a horse as my biggest problem. The pressures of life always seemed to press down on me and keep me a bundle of nerves. Mom's unpredictable anger toward me and my brother seemed to grow every year. Constantly hovering over us was like a plastic bag, always threatening to suck the air out of my lungs. Being Bill's boy could be fun, but it was still demanding. Rick and Todd still came to get me once a week. It seemed there was always somebody I had to be ready to please. The things I wanted to do fell to the bottom of the list and never seemed to get done.

Dad knocked on my door really hard and scared me, "Timmy, who's Joey?"

"Just a kid from school"

"He's on the phone for you. Make it quick. I'm expecting a call."

As I passed Dad, he told me, "I need you to run to the store for me."

"Sure, Dad" I answered the phone. "Hey, Joey, what's going on?"

"Timmy," his voice was really excited.

I heard Brian's voice also; he was on another extension.

"Is anyone else listening?" Brian asked.

"No."

"I need to meet with you, but I don't want anyone else to know."

"Okay, when?"

"What about tomorrow?"

I hesitated because I really wanted to go to Mark's house.

"What do you have to do tomorrow?"

"Nothing disappointment sounding in my voice even though a part of me was glad to spend time with Brian and was hoping everything was alright between us.

"Good. I'll pick you up after school."

"Okay."

Dad told me to get milk, root beer and vanilla ice cream so Mom could make root beer floats after dinner.

I had to make some calls at the pay phone by the store. I was bummed out that I was going to have to cancel with Mark. But I figured I could still get over there Wednesday or Thursday. When I called, he sounded disappointed, but he picked Wednesday for me to come over.

Next I had to call Bill and just check in because he liked to hear from me about every other day if I wasn't at his house. He told me he had a surprise for me, but he couldn't see me until Friday.

At school the next day went by so slow because I was looking forward to seeing Brian. I spent a lot of time wondering why Brian had called and what he wanted from me. When the bell rang, I walked to the store to meet Brian. I was surprised when Roger drove up. I hadn't been looking for his car. If I had spotted him first, I would have hidden before he saw me. I never knew what to expect out of Roger. And since I had hit Carlos, I wasn't sure if this was a revenge thing. Before I would get in, I made Roger roll down the window and talk to me.

Roger asked, "What's wrong?"

"Are you mad at me?"

"No. I'm not." Roger sounded frustrated.

"Where's Carlos?"

"Timmy, just get in!"

"You're not going to kick my ass are you?"

"No! But you better get in before I change my mind! I got in the car and pursued my line of questioning, "Why aren't you mad?"

"Because I'm not just mad I'm more than pissed with you! You only did it because you knew Bill would protect you."

"That's not why, Roger. I just lost my temper."

"Do you hate Carlos now?'

"No! He's still my friend."

"Why haven't you called him?"

"I guess I'm scared."

"You don't have to be scared of Carlos. He would never hurt you."

"What do you think he will do to me when he sees me?"

"Well, you're about to find out?"

"Is he over at Brian's house?"

"No. He's at my house, and we're stopping there first before we go to Brian's."

I was trying to stay calm. This whole situation could get out of control very easily. "Did Brian set me up?"

"What the hell do you mean by that? Brian doesn't know anything about this! No one is setting you up! Damn! You sure know how to piss me off! I was silent for a minute and then told him I was sorry. We got to his house a few minutes later. Roger pulled into the driveway and honked his horn. Carlos came running out and smiling at me.

He opened the front door and I slid over. He put his arm around me and said, "Timmy, I'm sorry."

"Me too Carlos" I felt such relief that we could go back to being friends again.

Roger asked me, "Do you trust anyone?"

I wanted to answer that I used to trust Brian, but that would only make Roger angry. I realized that I couldn't think of anyone I could fully trust.

My silence lasted so long that Carlos asked me again, "Timmy, is there anyone?"

I looked at him and quickly answered correctly, "Of course, Carlos. I know I can trust you."

We all laughed and changed the subject to lighten the mood. We arrived at Brian's house before he got home. I went to my old room, but seeing it made me jealous. At Bill's house, I had an unused janitor's closet to store my things. I could use any guest bedroom, but I knew I was a paid servant in a modern kind of way. At Brian's,

I'd felt like we had been a family—something I'd missed out on even in my own home. I decided I had better join the guys before I got too sad.

I walked into the living room, and immediately, Roger and Carlos quit talking. "Am I interrupting a private conversation?" I asked.

Carlos looked a little shocked and said, "Wow! You've grown a set of balls."

Roger replied, "They aren't his. They're Bill's!"

I just turned and went back into the bedroom. I felt so out of place. I lay on the bed and closed my eyes. I felt someone bump the bed, and I looked up to see Joey standing there. We smiled at each other and the next thing I knew, he jumped on me. We wrestled a little, and I let him win for the fun of it. When he had me pinned to the bed, he leaned over my face and started letting spit string down from his mouth. I was yelling for him to stop, and when it got close he sucked it up.

When we got done horsing around, Joey sat next to me and said, "You're here for me."

"Why?"

"Well my dad, Brian, and Roger are all mad at me because I don't want to do the things they want me to."

"Oh, I get it."

"Timmy, how do you do it?"

"I gave up a long time ago."

"But you're happy."

I couldn't believe I was having this conversation. So I tried to explain as best I could. "When you give in, then you can learn to accept it. At times, it can be exciting and even fun, and the money isn't bad. The guys want to hang around you and tell you how great you are, and they give you cool gifts."

"Do you like doing it?"

"No, well sometimes I guess." It was hard to explain because I had trouble convincing myself that I actually knew why I did it.

"I like Carlos and Troy, but they aren't like you."

I was confused so I asked, "what do you mean?'

He looked kind of shy and then leaned over and kissed me on the lips.

I jerked my head back and wiped my face and asked, "What the hell are you doing?"

"Don't you want to?"

"No."

"Why not" It's not like we haven't done it before."

"That's because I was told to."

"See, Timmy, that's why you're different. Everybody else wants to screw me every time I turn around."

Then I understood that Joey and I were a lot alike. The only exception was that he had more guts than I did. And if he didn't want to do something, he fought every step of the way. I knew his way would only bring him pain and unhappiness because this group would always find a way to break you. Since his dad was involved, he didn't have any way to escape.

Joey asked me, "Did you know they have pictures of me?"

"Yeah"

Angrily he asked, "Why? Did you see them?"

Patiently I replied, "No, Joey, because they do that to all of us."

"I know. I've even seen one of your movies.'

"Well shit, Joey, you get mad that I might have seen a picture of you, but you've seen a movie with me in it. That's a lot worse."

"It made me want to be in one."

"Brian will never let you."

"Yes he will. He told me that's what he wants."

"That doesn't sound like the Brian that I knew."

"He's going along because everyone else wants it too."

"Who"

"I heard him say Bill, Roger, and even my own dad. He just wants the money."

"Joey, why am I really here today? Do you know? Don't lie to me."

"We are waiting for my dad because he wants to meet you."

"Come on, Joey, what is really going on?"

He reached into his pocket and pulled out a pill.

"What is that?" I asked.

"Brian calls it an 'I don't care pill.'"

"Oh shit, Joey! Who gave this to you?"

"Brian, why"

"Shit! Shit! Shit!" I kept chanting. "Did you set me up?"

"No! I swear!"

"Are they going to hurt me?"

"I don't think so."

"Bullshit, Joey! If Brian thinks I need a pill, I'm screwed!" I took the pill out of his hand and swallowed it. I lie down and felt horrible. I thought I was going to throw up. I knew what had happened in the past when they'd drugged me, and it was way past anything my mind could handle.

Joey left the room and brought back Roger. The pill was starting to take effect. Roger walked me into the bathroom and wiped my face with a wet cloth. He was talking, but I wasn't listening.

Then he looked at me and asked, "What did he give you?"

"Just a pill"

"What did it look like?"

"I don't remember," I said. I was feeling great, and I hoped it would get even better.

"Oh shit! Well than we've got to get started."

We walked to the garage, and everyone was already there. Joey was standing next to his dad, and even with my blurring vision, I could see how much they looked alike. Brian had done a lot of work to his garage. With a new, upgraded S and M room, Brian wasn't going to leave his garage door open for the neighbors to see.

They had a movie camera set up some racks that I had never seen before.

Joey walked up to me and asked, "How are you feeling?"

"A little weird"

"Take your shirt off," Joey instructed.

As I took mine off, I noticed his was already off. Removing my shirt wasn't the easiest feat with the pills in my system. I felt like I was there, but then again I felt really far away.

Joey walked me over to the new version of the wooden rack. By the time Joey was tying me down on the rack I noticed I was naked and didn't remember how I got that way.

The next thing I could actually comprehend was waking up in Brian's bed. I still didn't have any clothes on and felt like I had been torn apart. I had felt pain before, but this was a new level for me. I moved slightly and screamed in pain. I was lying on my stomach with my head at the foot of the bed. When I looked at the floor, I saw a bowl and washcloth and a lot of blood in both.

It was then that I noticed Carlos was wiping me off and cleaning me up. Hearing me cry out, he walked in front of me and knelt down and asked, "How do you feel?"

"How do I look?" I asked with tears in my eyes.

"Not bad," he lied.

There was a sheet lying next to me, and I rolled so I could cover myself in it before I kept talking. "I thought you weren't mad at me?"

"What are you talking about? This had nothing to do with you and me. I never touched you."

"Well who did?"

"You were there too, Timmy. Why are you asking me?"

"Carlos, I took a pill, and I don't remember anything. Was it Joey's dad?"

Yeah! And everyone else in the room it was the craziest thing I have ever seen."

I rolled slowly out of bed, taking in this new information. I put my feet on the floor and kept the sheet wrapped around me and stood up slowly. I was dizzy and groggy from the medicine still. I walked into the bathroom and turned on the lights, which made my head hurt even worse. I looked in the mirror and saw that I had a huge fat lip. Before I could check the rest of myself, I asked Carlos, "Who did this to me?"

"Joey's dad," He answered without any explanation.

I was confused about why he wanted to hurt me. But first, I needed to see where else I was hurt. I dropped the sheet and looked at my backside in the mirror. There weren't any whip marks but my legs and butt were bright red. "I thought someone had whooped the shit out of me."

"No Timmy, but that would have been better for you. They screwed the hell out of you. I didn't know a human body could be bent in that many positions."

That was the worst kind of news I could have heard. I bent down to pick up the sheet once again, and horrible pain shot up in my groin. It felt like I had been kicked really hard in the balls. I looked down and they were swollen to twice the normal size. Confused at all the different kinds of injuries, I asked Carlos, "Did someone kick me in the balls?"

"Hello, Timmy, you were there! Why do you keep asking all these questions?"

I looked at him confused and asked, "Wasn't I knocked out?"

"No. Are you kidding? You really don't remember anything?"

I stopped and thought really hard. "If I concentrate, I can remember bits and pieces, but it is just a blur."

Carlos could see I was telling the truth and asked incredulously, "You aren't kidding are you?"

"No. Joey gave me a pill, and everything is fuzzy after that."

"What kind of pill?"

"I don't know."

"And you took it?"

"I thought Brian had Joey give it to me. It wouldn't be the first time."

Carlos stormed out of the room and went to get Brian and Roger. I wrapped up in the sheet and went to lie back down on the bed, exhausted from all my efforts.

Brian walked in with a look on his face that reminded me of the old days. "Damn you're cute," he said.

Roger just moaned like hearing that put him in pain and asked, "What did Joey give you?"

"Just one pill" And I took it because I thought you guys wanted me to. Just ask Joey. He'll tell you."

They both left the room looking angry.

Carlos said, "Joe and Joey left already."

"Is that his dad's name?"

"Yeah"

We both laughed.

I laid my head back and closed my eyes, knowing there wasn't anything more I could do now and sleep sounded good to me. I kept seeing strange things and parts of weird conversations. I didn't say anything to Carlos because it would be too hard to try to explain. He seemed to come and go a lot as I slept.

I even had a horrible nightmare that I was back in the garage tied to the rack. My dad walks in. I can't move and run and hide because I am tied down. He yells at me and says how ashamed he is and that I couldn't be his son. I was the biggest disappointment that he could imagine.

I pulled myself out of this nightmare because I couldn't handle this on top of everything else going on. I came awake yelling to Carlos, "My dad is here."

Patiently, Carlos explained that it was a nightmare and wiped my face off with a cold washcloth. I wanted to go back to sleep, but I was too afraid I couldn't control my mind.

Brian came through the door yelling at me, "This is your entire fault!" He kept yelling and cussing and then disappeared before my eyes.

I started crying and asked Carlos what was happening.

"You're having hallucinations."

"Why would they give that to me?"

"They didn't, Timmy. It was just Joey."

I fell back to sleep, trying to reason all this out. I woke up in my own bed, not remembering how I got there. I had a dozen dreams and none of them made any sense. I looked at the clock, and it was 10:00 am. No one had gotten me up for school. I was still really sore, and I rolled out of bed to get dressed. I noticed I was naked, and that was really weird because I never slept that way.

I got dressed and walked quietly through the house to see if anyone was home. Mom was gone, and a note on the counter said she was at her parents' house for the day. I couldn't believe how lucky I was.

I called Carlos's house, and Roger answered and told me he was in school. "Why aren't you in school? And why did you call from your home phone?! You know you aren't ever supposed to do that! What's wrong with you? "I was hoping Carlos could tell me. Can you?"

"No!"

"Okay, I have to go."

"Do you need me to come get you?"

"No."

We hung up. Then before I could leave the kitchen, the phone began to ring again. I figured it was Roger, but I couldn't take a chance that it was Mom.

After it quit ringing, I called Mark at home. I was surprised that he answered the phone.

"Hi, Mark, this is Timmy."

I could tell he was glad to hear from me, but then he asked, "Aren't you supposed to be in school?"

I paused for a minute and decided to answer honestly, "I don't know."

"Timmy, you can't keep ditching school."

"I know you haven't known me for long, but I'm telling the truth when I say I don't normally ditch school."

"Are you sick?"

'I don't know, maybe. I feel funny."

"Timmy, what's wrong?"

"Nothing, everything, I don't know. I just called to tell you I can't meet with you today."

"Why? Are you in trouble?"

"I don't think so."

"Where are you?"

"At home"

"Are your parents there?"

"No."

"Do they know your home?"

"No."

"Good. I'm coming over to get you. Do you expect them home anytime soon?"

"No."

"I'll be there in fifteen minutes."

I agreed because, for some reason, I felt I could trust him. I sat down on the couch and closed my eyes for a minute. The next thing I heard was a knock on the door and looked and saw it was Mark.

Mark asked, "Are you ready?"

Yeah. How did you get here so fast?"

He looked at me funny and answered, "It took half an hour."

I just shook my head in wonder and got in the car.

"What's wrong, Timmy? And why are you walking funny?"

"If I tell you, you have to swear you won't tell anyone. It has to stay between us."

Mark assured me that he would stay quiet. I told him what had happened, leaving nothing out—as much as I had pieced together. It sounded crazy even to me.

"Wow. That's quite a story."

"You don't believe me, do you?"

"Yeah, I believe you."

"Good, because I swear to God it's the truth."

We arrived at his house and went inside. He offered me a Coke, and I took it. We sat at the kitchen table and talked. I did most of the talking, and Mark kept asking questions when I ran out of stuff to say. I really liked that. The last person who had listened and acted like he cared like that was Brian. Mark offered to go horseback riding with me, but I knew I hurt too badly to sit on a horse.

We decided a game of checkers would be fun. After that, he started teaching me how to play chess. When we both got hungry, we went into the kitchen and Mark showed me how to make a homemade pizza.

Mark asked, "You aren't going to tell Bill you were here today are you?"

"No."

"Won't he want to know where you've been?"

"No. Not as long as I show up when he wants me to."

"What about your parents?"

"What about them?"

"Don't they care who you are with?"

"Not as long as I spend just enough time there."

"Don't they ask questions?"

"Why would they? I've never been in any trouble that they know of."

"So they have no idea . . ."

"About what" I asked sounding innocent but playing with him on purpose.

"You know." he didn't want to have to say the words out loud.

"No. I don't. What are you talking about?" Then I smiled at him and added, "No. They don't know anything about that."

After we ate and played some more board games, he took me back to the stores near my house so I could walk home. As he dropped me off, I asked, "When will I see you again?"

He smiled and asked back, "When can you?"

"I'll call you tomorrow."

I went to the pay phone and called home. Tommy answered and told me that Mom would be at her parents' house until later tonight. He also said that Carlos and Joey had both called for me. I thanked him and hung up.

I called Brian's house first to talk to Joey.

Brian answered and asked, "How are doing, Timmy?" his voice sounding concerned.

"Not too good."

"What's wrong?"

"It doesn't matter. Is Joey there?"

"What do you mean it doesn't matter?"

"You know damn good and well what I'm talking about! The Brian I used to know would never have let anyone do what they did to me last night!" The saddest part was I still wasn't completely sure what had happened. Between my nightmares, my flashbacks, and my hallucinations, I probably would never really know how bad it had been.

"Timmy, what do you think happened to you?" Brian asked tentatively.

"I'm on a phone. Do you really want to talk about this?"

"No, you're right. Where are your parents?"

"Out"

"Are you at home or at the drugstore?"

"I'm at the drugstore."

"Stay there. I'll be there in twenty minutes, and then we can talk."

I agreed, hoping that maybe I could get to the bottom of this. I called Carlos next, and Roger answered the phone.

"Is Carlos there?"

Roger covered the phone and called Carlos's name.

We talked for a few minutes, but he wasn't giving up any information, so I just gave up. I knew I didn't really want to meet with Brian. Things could never be the same. He wasn't going to protect me or watch out for me or help these wounds heal. Time had passed, and we had both changed. Once again, I was faced with that reality.

I walked home slowly, my mind jumping from good times to some really horrible events. I couldn't remember back to a time when I'd just been a carefree kid. I felt old and used and unsure of how to change any of it.

My brother was gone when I got home, so I fixed a nice, hot bubble bath and soaked in the tub until the water turned cold. Then I put on an oversize T-shirt and figured I would just go to sleep early.

The phone rang, and I answered it Brian's voice sounded angry. "Timmy, I waited forty-five minutes for you! We needed to talk about this. Why didn't you wait for me?"

I was silent, not sure how to put my feelings into words.

The silence lasted long enough that he yelled, "Answer me!"

Thinking quickly I lied, "Brian, my mom needs the phone."

"Is she there?"

"Yes."

"Oh shit! Did she hear me?"

"No."

"Okay, bye."

I went to my room to lie down. It was only 5:30, but it was getting dark outside. And my body needed the rest. Before I could fall asleep, the phone began to ring again. The person just kept letting it ring and I was afraid that it could be mom checking up on us. I got up and answered, "Hello?"

"Timmy, is that you?" Tyler asked.

"Yeah"

"What took you so long?"

Without giving an answer, I just said, "Sorry."

"Dad wants you to come over after school tomorrow."

"Last I heard he didn't want me over until Friday. He said something about a surprise."

"I don't know anything about that. Can you come over tomorrow?"

"Yeah"

"See you tomorrow." He hung up before I could ask him for a ride.

I went back to bed and fell asleep quickly. I must have slept hard because I didn't hear Tommy or anyone come home. I woke up before the alarm and rode my bike to school. I rode straight to Tyler's house after school; it was really painful riding my bike. Every turn was torcher and it was really cold and the wind was blowing. By the time I got there, I was cold to the bone.

I didn't see any of their cars in the garage and realized no one was home yet. I needed to get warm fast, so I went straight to the Jacuzzi and stripped down and got in. The water was just the temperature that I liked it, and I began to warm up quickly. I wasn't there very long before Tyler came walking in. He stripped off his clothes and got in also.

"I looked all over the house for you."

"I was really cold from riding my bike over here. I needed to warm up. Is your dad here?"

"No. He called and said he wouldn't be home tonight."

"Really I thought he wanted me to come over."

"No. Not really."

"That's what you said last night on the phone."

"I told you that so you would come over. I missed you."

"I would have come over just the same for you, Tyler."

"Really"

"Yeah"

This made him smile. We talked a little and then started telling jokes. I only knew a few, but Tyler knew a lot. They were crude but really funny to such a young kid

I knew why I was really here. It wasn't for the jokes or the friendship. It was for other reasons. Actually, Tyler was right; I didn't know if I would have come over just for him. I would rather have gone (horseback) riding at Mark's than to have to service Tyler.

Tyler finally quit talking and started to make his move. He was still nervous and unsure at this stage. We ended up in his room and I noticed he did things differently this time. I could take the pain, but still screamed because of it. This only excited Tyler When it was over and I asked him, "Where did you learn to do that?"

"Why? Hasn't anyone ever done that to you before?"

I just looked at him not answering.

Finally he said, "Carlos taught me."

That confirmed what I had been thinking for a while.

Tyler asked, "Why? Are you jealous?"

"No. Not at all"

"Dad told me if I saw him again he would beat us both half to death, Take away my Porsche, and ground me until Jesus comes back."

"Why? What happened? Did you get caught?"

"Kind of at my party, things got out of hand. You don't need to know the details!

Things were making sense to me now. Bill had been extremely mad at Carlos, and that was what his beating was for at the last party. Then I got in a fight with Carlos and had to be corrected, but Bill wanted Carlos's punishment to be sufficient. Now I was glad that Bill had made me leave with him the night of the party.

"Are you hungry?" Tyler asked.

"I'm starved," I replied.

As Tyler left for the kitchen, I went to the locker room and got some clothes. I took a quick shower and headed for the kitchen. I could smell the food, and my stomach started growling. It didn't take me long to eat my hamburger and all the fries he put on my plate.

"Do you want a ride home?' Tyler asked.

That was a nice surprise. He usually didn't care how I got home.

"Thanks, but I rode my bike, and it won't fit in your Porsche."

"That's no problem. I'll take one of the trucks."

"Great! Thanks."

When Tyler dropped me off, it was still early—about 4:30. He drove into the driveway, and before I got out he said, "I'll see you tomorrow."

"You will?"

"Yes, you're coming over aren't you?"

"Yeah I just didn't think you would be there. What is the surprise, Tyler?" I tried, knowing he wouldn't give it away.

"You'll see," he answered, driving away smiling.

Surprise

I walked in the house. Mom was lying down with a migraine, and Dad was out of town. I fixed myself something to eat, stayed in my room, and went to bed early.

The next day went by surprisingly quickly. The teachers were getting ready for parent-teacher conferences, and it was more like a play day. We were off the whole next week, and we couldn't wait to start school vacation.

Ms. Right called me up front before the final bell rang and said, "I haven't been able to reach your mom all week. She is the only one I haven't been able to set an appointment with. I need you to give her this note."

I nodded my head and put the note in my pocket. I was thinking that the biggest favor I could do for Ms. Right was to throw this note away. My mom probably wouldn't show up anyways, but if she did, it wouldn't be a good meeting at all for Ms. Right. My mom had a way of making enemies with most people.

The bell rang, and I rode to Bill's house in record time. I ran into the kitchen yelling, "I'm here!"

A voice on the intercom came back asking, "Who is it?" Bill knew who it was, but this was fun.

"It's me!" I said, pushing the button to talk on the intercom.

"Who's me"

"It's me, Bill, Timmy!"

I could hear his laughter.

"I'll be down in a minute."

I heard him coming down the stairs and headed that way. He was smiling at me, and I knew this was my cue to run and give him a hug. I ran past him a couple of steps, and he turned around to see what was going on. When he turned, I jumped into his arms and hugged his neck real tight.

"I've missed you," Bill said as he hugged me back.

"Where have you been?" I asked.

"Nowhere special"

"Really I thought you left the country or something."

"No. I've had a lot of work at the office, and I've been working on a project here at home."

"What project?"

"You'll have to wait and see. Tyler is out of school next week. Are you?"

"Yeah"

"Good."

We walked into the family room, and he wanted to know what I had been up to. I knew now was the time if I was going to tell him what had happened at Brian's house. I knew he would find a way to take care of it, but I had kept so many secrets all along that I found it hard to start talking now. I always knew that the adults all had pictures and movies that they could blackmail me with. And above all other, things I couldn't stand the thought that my family or classmates would find out what I had done. So I kept the silence and the loyalty to this group about one more bizarre instance in my life. Instead, I made up some kid stuff that sounded good and made it sound like I had stayed busy.

There was a knock at the front door, and I looked at Bill. He wasn't getting up. "Go answer it," he told me.

I opened the door, and it was Roger, Carlos, Rick, Todd, and Troy. I had a sinking feeling that this wasn't going to be a good surprise for me if the group had to be there. Troy was the only one I was glad to see, but I put on a fake smile and let them all in. I told them that Bill was in the family room, and everyone but Troy went to talk to Bill.

My face lit up genuinely when I turned to Troy. "Why are we here, Timmy?" he asked me.

"I don't know. I didn't even know you guys were coming over. But now that you are here, my only guess is that they want to make some more movies."

"Do you really think so?"

"All the right people are here."

As we entered the room where the men were he looked at the group and agreed. I looked at Troy and noticed that his hair was even longer. Even though he was in that preteen age, he was really good-looking.

The doorbell rang again and I opened it. This time it was Brian and Joey. Brian reached down to hug me, and I hugged him back. He went to the family room with the other adults. Joey stood there and started to hug me, but I was still mad about him giving me the pill and I pulled away.

Joey turned and started walking away with his head down.

I felt bad that I had reacted like that and asked, "Where are you going?"

He turned back and asked, "Are you mad at me?"

"No. I guess not," I answered.

Then Bill called for all us boys to come to the family room. He had us follow him down the hallway, past his office and game room, to the door that he always kept locked. It was Bill's torture room, I had only been in there a few times, and I had never wanted to Return. Bill pulled out the keys to unlock the door, and a sickening feeling creeping in the pit of my stomach and Goosebumps spread all over my body. Bill pushed me gently so I would go in first. I couldn't believe that this was the surprise that I had been excited about for days. I couldn't believe that these adults didn't understand that the pain they inflicted on us only brought *them* pleasure and that every new party or movie scene had the potential to get out of hand—that someone could get really hurt. What happened to the old days when a surprise was a day at the beach or Disneyland? Some things I would never understand.

Bill had renovated and upgraded until this room looked like a professional movie set. Everything he did was the very best, but he'd outdone himself this time. Three movie cameras sat on tripods with wheels. Mirrors, props, lighting on wheels, an array of backdrops, and a dressing room with a bathroom completed the upgrade. Bill stood, looking completely proud of himself.

I looked at the others and saw that Rick, Todd, Roger, Carlos, and even Troy looked thrilled. Then I noticed that Brian, Joey, and I all had the same sick smile we hoped would pass for enthusiasm.

Bill looked at me and asked, "What's wrong, Timmy? Isn't this great?"

"Yeah" It's great!" I did my best to look and sound convincing, and it worked.

There was a pool table in the middle of the room, and I knew which movie they wanted us to remake first.

Rick pointed at me and Troy and said, "I need you two first."

He told us how it was going to play out and then handed us a script with our lines. This was new to us. But as we read it, we realized they had used the original dialogue with only a few minor changes.

Rick gave Carlos a script because he was going to be in the second scene. Rick went to talk to Roger and Bill because they would be on the cameras. Todd would be directing, and Brian and Joey would just be watching for now. Carlos approached Rick, upset that he wouldn't be in the first scene. Roger and Carlos had only gotten involved about six months ago. Rick and Todd had been doing these movies for a while.

"Why can't Carlos be in the first scene?" Roger asked when Rick didn't answer the first time.

"He just can't!" Rick said with authority. Realizing that this was not going to satisfy them both he finally added, "We know what sells."

I was sitting back watching all this, hoping that Carlos could take all my scenes, and I would get out of everything today.

"What do you mean you know what sells?! Carlos is perfect! He has a perfect body and a perfect face!" Roger argued.

"That has nothing to do with it," Rick tried to explain without stating the obvious.

"Is it because he is older?" Roger pressed.

"Partially" Rick knew they still wanted to use him in other parts of the movie.

"Then what's the rest of it?" Roger demanded.

"Every kid but Timmy is Latino. We've done this both ways, and if you put a white kid in, it sells twice as much. I don't know all the reasons. I just know the bottom line is we make a lot more money. Why do you think we worked so hard to get him back?" Rick said.

Carlos was so pissed that he left the room and never came back. It didn't matter anyways because the men were having trouble figuring out how to use the equipment. Troy and I played pool and stayed quiet so we didn't irritate anyone. After about two hours, they were all getting pissed off.

"We need a real producer," Bill finally said.

"Why?" Todd yelled, not wanting to get any more people involved in this private matter.

"Because we don't know what the hell we are doing. Even if we get the cameras working, we won't know how to edit the film correctly."

"Who then"

"Craig."

"I hate that arrogant, little bastard. He's criticized everything we've done."

"Because he knows what he's doing. That's what he does for a living."

They all ended up agreeing that getting Craig involved was the best option they had of making this work. So Bill left to go talk to him.

I took Joey and Troy to the game room since we didn't need to stay. We played a couple games of bowling before Brian came to get Joey. When they left, I asked Troy if he wanted to spend the night. I got permission from Bill and he got permission from his dad, and we were both glad to be able to hang out together.

We decided to go swimming and chose the inside pool so we could dive without getting cold every time we got out of the pool. Tyler showed up later, and he could really dive. He worked with me and Troy to teach us the technique. I picked it up pretty quickly, but Troy was having a little more trouble. Just when I thought I was getting pretty good, Tyler did a double flip off the board, and Troy and I stood amazed. We both said at the same time, "Well, that's not going to happen." Then we grabbed our towels, ready to call it a day.

Tyler called after us, "Trust me, you can do it. I'll show you."

Then Bill walked in. "It's time to eat."

"Saved," Troy said.

Bill had sent out for Chinese food. Tyler and Troy wasted no time sitting down and filling their plates. I was amazed at all the different cartons of food and how strange it all looked. Bill looked at me and asked, "What's wrong? Don't you like Chinese food?"

"I don't know. I've never had it before."

"Well, you're about to try something new. I'll put a little of everything on your plate, and you can see what you like."

I was surprised to find I liked several things a lot. It was a nice change not to have the food you hated shoved down your throat so your mom could be entertained. It reminded me once again why I preferred hanging out with these guys than staying at home.

Tyler and Troy and I stayed up late playing a cutthroat game of Monopoly. Tyler had his dad's business mind and finally beat us. Bill opened the door to tell us he was going to bed and warned, "No funny stuff, boy's"

Troy looked confused, but Tyler and I just nodded our heads in agreement.

We went to Tyler's room and piled on the bed and talked for a long time. I finally fell asleep about 2:00 am listening to Tyler and Troy talk.

I woke up first in the middle of the bed and moved cautiously so I didn't wake them. I walked down the stairs and could hear the men talking as I got near.

Todd saw me first and said, "It's already noon. I thought you were going to sleep all day."

I smiled, as I was rubbing my eyes and trying to clear my head.

Bill told me to take a shower and they were going to start filming in about an hour.

I looked around the room at all the people that were now involved in what used to be such a "secret event." This movie stuff had grown beyond just satisfying the guys in the group. I turned and headed for the gym to shower and change clothes.

Carlos followed me and called out, "Timmy, wait up."

Bill saw Carlos following me and yelled for him to come back. They had a few words, and all I could hear was "Don't touch him."

I was walking slowly so I could hear more.

Carlos ran to catch up to me and asked, "Why does everyone think I'm mad at you?"

"Aren't you?" I asked.

"No not at all I'm the one who cleaned you up the other night."

"Look, Carlos, I don't remember much about the other night—well, nothing I can make sense of anyways. I don't even know how I ended up in my own bed."

"You were pretty wasted."

"Why? Why did they want me wasted?"

"Don't ask me. I didn't give it to you. Joey did."

"But didn't Roger tell him to give it to me?"

"No, he stole it from his dad."

"Why?"

"You're going to have to ask him. I think he was embarrassed."

"About what"

"You're going to have to ask him all this."

We got to the locker room and I reached up under the pipe and got my key. Carlos commented that it was a good hiding place. That made me realize I would need a new one now. The metal shelves were full of toys and gifts that the men had given me. When my lock box was full I had to hide my money in other places in the desk drawer. My clothes were folded on one shelf, and I grabbed some to change into.

"You got a lot of stuff here. You must be making a lot of people happy."

I looked at him and we both started laughing.

He looked at my clothes and said, "Your taste really sucks. Let me go with you next time you go shopping."

"Really"

"Sure." He stared at me for a long time and we were both thinking about the days at Brian's house when we were all together. "Things aren't the same, we all miss you," Carlos said.

"Everyone"

"Yeah especially Brian"

"That made me feel a little better"

Carlos left to go to the movie studio and I took a shower. There were even more people today because Bill let Tyler stay to watch and Craig was showing the guys how to use the equipment.

Troy walked up to me and asked, "Do you think there are enough people here?"

"I was thinking the same thing," I answered.

Todd told me to start playing pool, and this began our first scene of the movie. It was strip pool. We were remaking the movie that we made at Rick and Todd's house, During Tyler's party it turn out really cheesy and the men weren't wearing mask to hide their Identity. Know the game was played the same and for every ball your opponent hit in, you had to take something off. We were halfway through the game when one of the guys noticed that Troy had put on two of everything. It was actually funny, but the guys were mad about the wasted time and film.

Bill got everyone back on track without being too hard on Troy. We started over again and got through the first scene without any interruptions. By the second scene, things were heating up for the men, especially Craig because he was new. He kept commenting that it was driving him crazy. Joey looked stunned and scared. Tyler was really enjoying himself. There were times we had to do things two and three times to get it right.

Finally, Todd called, "Cut." And that was all for today.

I turned for the door and ran to the pool. Troy was right behind me, and we both jumped in with a splash. It was time to feel clean again—and to try to feel young again.

Most of the others made their way to the pool a few minutes later. Joey took his shoes and socks off and put his feet in the pool. Troy and I encouraged him to just get in and swim with us. After a little hesitation, he stood up and took off his clothes and joined us. It wasn't long before everyone but Bill and Craig were in the pool. We played around for about an hour. Then Bill came out and told everyone to get out and dry off and come inside.

He had us sit in the family room, and I looked around at all the animals from his hunting trips that decorated the room. A large, stuffed bear stuffed menaced from the corner. A twelve-point deer looked out over the fireplace, and a moose head hung on the wall.

Bill called us to order. He pointed to a machine on top of his television and call it Beta max and said, "Mark my words; one day, every household in America will have one of these."

I did notice roger was holding a hand held device not like the other cameras.

Then he turned on the machine, and I thought I would faint. I looked at Troy, and he was as pale as I felt. "Holy shit" he said.

We were watching our uncut video. It was too much for me to watch on a TV. I looked away and felt sick. The men in the room were extremely happy with the movie. I hadn't eaten since last night, but I knew I was moments away from throwing up. I ran out of the room to the nearest bathroom and threw up.

I couldn't believe what I had just seen. It was grotesque, raw, and uncut. I didn't know that there was technology out there that could put a movie on your television. I made it back in time to hear the men clapping. But none of the boys were clapping.

Bill asked, "What's wrong?"

Carlos asked, "How did you do that?"

Bill explained, "We had three movie cameras, and one Beta max video camera."

Carlos asked, "Are you going to sell those?"

"No," Bill replied.

"Then what did you mean that they will be in every house?" Carlos was asking the questions that all of us boys wanted to know the answer to.

"I meant that someday the technology will improve and the Beta max players will be affordable and in every house."

Bill wasn't catching onto what we were afraid of most. This increased our risk of exposure greatly if what he said was true. Our old films could be shown in the living room of someone from our group. He was opening our eyes to the possibility of uncontrolled exposure.

I spoke up, "Bill, what about my parents? My friends! We don't want them getting a hold of this."

Bill yelled, "Time out! Stop! You guys don't understand what I'm saying. This tape is just for us! It will never be sold. I am talking about the bigger picture of technology upgrading our ability to watch any movie in our homes. You guys need to calm down."

Even though I heard and understood Bill, I had heard too many comments about "what sold", marketing, and clients. But I was too involved already, and there was no way someone like me could stop something this big.

The guys changed the subject and ordered pizza for us. We went for the pool while the men talked some more. In the pool Carlos, was trying to convince me that everything would be all right. He said, "They would never sell that movie to anyone."

"Why? "Because they are so honest with us" I asked sarcastically. There selling the other ones and there of poor quality! So why wouldn't they sell better one of a higher quality for more money?

"No because if the movie ever gets traced back to them then the game is up. All their fun is over."

It doesn't make any sense, but I added, "And our lives are ruined."

"Don't worry, Timmy. They would rather die than be exposed for having sex with young boys."

I knew he was wrong and was starting to feel sick again.

I never watched all the movies. I'd only seen two of them in the past two years, and I'd been forced to watch both of them. I didn't know how many movies were out there. I had been in at least a dozen of them before Nick was brought in. And it had been about a year before Carlos and Troy had gotten involved. I also knew there were an untold number of photographs of me and the other kids. I had to stop thinking about it, or I was going to get even sicker.

The pizza came, and after everyone got full, the men and boys all headed back to their houses for the night.

By Choice

With everyone gone, Bill, Tyler, and I sat around the table talking. Bill commented, "So Timmy, you have a week off from school."

"Doesn't everybody?" I asked.

"No, not every school"

"None of the other boys do, just you, which is perfect," Bill replied.

"Why?"

"Because none of the other boys were in the first movies just you" We need to set up some times so you and Rick and Todd can start filming."

I didn't want to spend my week off reenacting some of the worst moments of my life. Rick and Todd totally freaked me out back then. I wanted to be a kid and hang out with Mark and go horseback riding. I wanted to see some of my friends from school and do regular, fun things. But I didn't have the guts to say all of that to Bill, so I just changed the subject and asked, "Can I go home now?"

"Why?" Bill asked.

"Well if you are done with me, I need to get home."

"You haven't spent any time with me," Bill said, and I knew what he was referring to.

"It's not my fault. You've been too busy for me."

"Well, I'm not busy now."

I followed him to his bedroom, and when he was done, he paid me. I went back to my locker room and put all but a hundred dollars away. It was more than Bill would allow me to take home, but what he didn't know wouldn't hurt him. I sure as hell knew I'd earned every bit of my money. I changed clothes again and locked my room and found a new hiding place for the key.

Bill and Tyler were waiting for me and Bill asked, "Can you come back tomorrow?"

"But its Sunday," I said, surprised because usually he and Tyler took that day to hang out together.

"Why? Do you have some other plans?" Bill asked with a little attitude.

"I don't know. I have to check with my parents."

By this time, Bill had given my dad quite a few side jobs, really good paying ones too. He even introduced my dad to a famous baseball player, and Dad had done some work for him. I told him I would call him later with the answer. He had Tyler take me home, and I loved that because I got to ride in his Porsche.

I walked in the door and announced I was home. No one seemed to care, so I went to my room. I was trying to think of a way to get out of going to Bill's house. I stayed in my room until Mom called me for dinner. Neither of my parents had been drinking, and Mom cooked a really good dinner. It was a nice time, and no one was forcing food down my throat. I figured the timing was as good as it was going to get and asked if I could go to Tyler's house tomorrow.

Mom quickly said, "No!" and gave no reason.

After dinner, I had to call Bill and tell him I couldn't come over. When he asked why and I couldn't explain, he asked to talk to my dad.

I yelled, "Dad, the phone's for you."

"Who is it?"

"It's Bill."

Dad took the phone from me and started talking. I went to my room, and I was scared I was going to get into trouble. I turned on the stereo and laid on the bed waiting for the verdict. I was hoping Mom wouldn't take Bill's call as undermining her authority.

I had been right to be scared. Bill had talked my dad into letting me come over. That made Mom madder than hell. She came to my room with a newly made whip and yelled, "So you called your friend's dad to have your dad override me. When I tell you no, I mean it. You don't go over my head to get what you want!"

I tried to explain, but hearing my voice only made her madder. The first swing brought the whip across my face. It stung horribly. I covered my face with my hands, and she aimed for my back. She was swinging fast, and I couldn't protect myself fast enough. I was screaming in pain, hoping that would make her stop. She grabbed me by my hair and pulled me off the bed so she could have more body parts to hit.

After a couple of hits, I heard the door open and Dad saying, "That's enough! Come to bed!"

I just lay there while she walked out. She told me to clean the kitchen before I went to bed. The whip marks hurt so badly I thought I would die. I lay there trying to calm down from crying so hard. I dreamed, I wished; I had prayed her dead for so long. I was even bored of thinking of new ways to kill her.

I knew I had to clean the kitchen, so I made myself get up. It hurt to stand, but I walked over to the dresser and looked in the mirror to check the damage. I had a fat lip and a red mark that might fade or might stay for a while. I lifted up my shirt, and it wasn't nearly as bad as it felt. I went to the kitchen and noticed she had started cleaning already, so it wasn't too bad.

I was almost done when she came in and said, "I've changed my mind. You can go see your friend tomorrow. He will be here at 7:00 am" she said sarcastically. "But so help me God, you ever go behind my back again, and I'll beat the hell out of you." Then she went back to her room to watch TV with Dad.

I went straight to bed and set my alarm for 6:30 a.m. I had no idea why Bill wanted me over tomorrow, but it had to be better than staying around here and getting another beating. I just wished there were times like I had with Brian and I got to hang out and have fun and just be a kid—times that had nothing to do with pleasing people, satisfying the men from the group, or starring in a film.

Close the Deal

It was exactly 7:00 am when Bill pulled into the driveway. I was dressed and ready, and my parents were still in bed. I walked to the car a little slower than usual because it hurt. Bill took one look at me and asked, "What the hell happened to you?"

I explained the story, and it made him mad. But that didn't really help because there was nothing he could do about it.

We went back to his house, and I saw Richard's car in the driveway. That was cool because it meant Troy was probably there too.

"What's up?" I asked.

"You and Troy are going to help me close a deal."

I had no idea what he meant by that.

Troy opened my car door and gave me a big hug.

We went into the house, and I asked Troy, "Do you know what's going on?"

"I don't have a clue," Troy said.

"All I know is that Bill said we would help him close a deal."

Neither of us was sure what deal he meant, so we went off to the game room to play. Bill caught us before we got to the door and asked, "Where are you guys going?"

I shrugged my shoulders and answered, "Nowhere."

"Well get in the car. We have a long drive ahead of us."

The Mercedes was in the driveway, and Richard was already in the passenger seat. Troy and I got in the backseat. We started the drive just talking about kid stuff while Richard and Bill were in deep conversation in the front seat.

"If I tell you something, can you keep it a secret?" I asked Troy, knowing it shouldn't be a problem with all the other secrets I already kept. I told Troy I would tell him a secret first.

He liked the idea and smiled and answered, "Yes."

I told him about my friend, Mark, and the horses and going to the beach with him. It was easy talking to Troy, and days like this made me forget what had made our paths cross.

Troy asked Bill, "Where are we going?"

"We are going to San Diego," Bill answered.

"What for" Troy asked.

"To help me close a deal"

"What does that mean?"

"You'll see."

I was sitting behind Bill so I reached up and massaged his shoulders for him, and he really liked that. The only reason I knew how to do that was because my mom made us give her shoulders rubs and feet rubs. Once you got started, there was no telling how long she would make you do it. If it wasn't good enough, she would reach out and slap your face. That was incentive enough to do it right the first time.

"Are we going to stop and eat?" I asked Bill. "Because I am starved"

"Yes, there's a place in about ten more minutes where I planned to stop," Bill answered.

When we pulled off the freeway, we pulled into a parking lot under a sign that said "Mom & Pop's Restaurant." I thought this was odd because this wasn't the kind of place that Bill usually went to.

He looked around the car and said, "Don't knock it. It's the best food you will ever eat."

"How did you find it?" I asked.

"I've been coming out here since I was a kid."

We walked in the door, and there was a sign informing us to seat ourselves. That wasn't easy either; the place was packed. I guess Bill wasn't the only one who liked the food.

A heavyset older woman came out of the back and ran to Bill when she saw him, exclaiming, "Boy, where have you been?'"

Bill stood up and gave her a big hug.

She yelled over her shoulder, "Tom, Robert is here."

He's a short old fat bald man and gave Bill a big hug.

I was smart enough not to react when I heard them call Bill by his real name.

Bill introduced Mom and Pop to everyone at our table. "Business looks good," he commented.

"Yeah, thanks to you," Pop answered, smiling.

"That was a long time ago," Bill replied. "This is a success because of you guys."

"We owe it all to you" Pop added.

"What will it be?" Mom asked, taking out a pad on which to write our drink down with than or orders.

"We'll all have your special," Bill told her.

"And it will be extra special when we get done with it," Mom said, smiling at Bill.

She and Pop both headed for the kitchen.

Troy was looking confused, and I was afraid that I knew why. I didn't have a chance to explain before he burst out, "Why did she call you Robert?"

I kicked him under the table, and he yelled. Bill gave him a look that should have told him to shut up. I looked at Troy and started talking to divert his attention. Bill and Richard started their own conversation also.

Troy leaned over and said real low, "What's wrong?"

"Bill doesn't use his real name," I explained.

"Why?"

"Most of the guys in the group don't use their real names, and they never use their last names. Didn't you ever know that?"

"No. Why? I don't understand?"

"We'll talk about this later, Troy."

"Okay."

Bill and Richard stopped talking just as we did and stared at us to make sure everything was under control.

I told Bill, "I need to go to the bathroom."

"So do I. Troy added" When we got inside Troy asked me, "Why don't they use their real names?"

I really did have to use the bathroom, but I knew that the sooner I answered the questions the better off Troy would be. Because they don't want us to know their real names haven't you noticed that, in the movies, they wear leather masks to cover their faces?"

"Why?"

"Are you kidding?! They don't want to get caught doing what they are doing. Just like you and Richard don't tell your mom what you guys are doing. How do you keep it from her?"

Troy dropped his head and said in a low voice, "She left"—he paused—"a long time ago. It's been about six months."

"Really" I'm sorry, I didn't know." I felt really bad for him.

"She didn't even tell us she was leaving. She just left without me, and we haven't heard anything from her."

"I'm sorry."

"No big deal."

We both finished in the bathroom and washed our hands. There was an empty cup on the sink, and I picked it up and starting filling it up.

"Ready to go back"

Troy asked.

"I am, but you're not," I said and then threw the water on him. "You need to dry off first." I laughed as I ran out the door. I slowed down before I got to the table.

"Where's Troy?" Richard asked.

"He got wet and has to dry off."

"What" Bill asked.

Just then, Troy made it back to the table, and Bill demanded, "What in the hell happened to you?"

"Yeah, What in the hell happened to you" I mimicked and smiled at him before he could answer Bill.

We were saved by the food being brought to the table.

Troy leaned over and whispered in my ear, "Payback is a bitch."

I just smiled and said, "You were getting sad, and I had to change your mood."

He understood then why I'd done it, but he would probably still try to get me later.

Our plates were piled high with eggs, biscuits, gravy, sausage, and bacon—much more than we could ever eat. Mom showed up and said, "Eat! Eat!" And I did with the vengeance of a starving kid.

I only made a dent in the plate and was completely full. It was the best breakfast I had ever tasted. I know now why the place was so packed. Troy and I joked around during breakfast, and sometimes the guys even joined in.

When it was time to go, I headed for the door as Bill went to pay. I heard Mom tell him, "Don't even think of it! Your money isn't any good around here." Then she hugged him and told him not to stay away so long.

We drove about another forty-five minutes and pulled up in front of a very expensive-looking hotel on the beach. We drove to the front door under an awning, and before I could reach for the door, someone opened it up for me. Another man met Bill, and Bill gave the man some money to take care of the car. Bill unlocked the trunk, and both men took some luggage out of the trunk. I was surprised because I didn't know we had any luggage. I knew nothing about this trip. I didn't know what to expect. Bill told us to sit down on one of the couches as he registered at the hotel.

"Troy, did you pack a bag?"

"Yeah, but I thought I was staying at Bill's house tonight."

"I didn't pack anything." I was very curious about what this adventure was about.

We followed the men and some bellhops that were carrying our stuff down a long hallway. At the end were two huge, wooden doors that the bellhops opened up to reveal the fanciest hotel room I had ever seen. It had a full living room, two bedrooms, a very large television, a full bar, and snack foods.

Bill pointed to Richard to show him which bedroom would be theirs, and Bill and I walked into our room. It was very nice, not quite as fancy as Bill's, but impressive still.

Bill called Troy into the room and handed us both some swim trunks and said, "Put these on. You guys can go swimming until we come and get you. Don't leave and go running around. Be sure you stay at the pool."

We both agreed and went and put our suits on.

As we were running out of the bedroom I heard Bill yell, "Timmy, come here!"

I didn't know what I had done to get into trouble already.

"What is that?" he asked, pointing to my back.

He was referring to the welts on my back and legs. I had forgotten about them because they didn't hurt that much. "I told you my mom got a hold of me last night." It wasn't nearly as bad as I'd had in the past. Dad had stopped Mom before she could do real damage.

He reached down and handed me a t—shirt I had just taken off and said, "You're going to have to wear this." He paused and looked at me with concern. "Was this my fault?"

I smiled reassuringly at him and answered, "My mom doesn't need a reason."

He tried to smile back and said, "I'm sorry. I'll make it up to you. Now go swimming and have a good time."

I ran quickly past Troy yelling, "Come on. Let's go."

We ended up having the pool to ourselves, and we could be as wild as we wanted. It was great to feel so carefree. Richard came down about 3:00 p.m. and it was good timing because we were getting really hungry. As we followed Richard back to the room, we were mimicking his every step. When he stopped to see what we were doing, we would stop. But of course it didn't take him long to get mad at this kind of screwing around.

Back in the room, Bill told us to rinse off and get dressed and informed us we were going to the mall. I thought this day was all about us having a good time, and it was a great treat—until Troy asked when were we going to eat again and Bill told us not until later that night. I knew then that Troy and I had work to do because they never let us eat before we had to entertain people. I looked over at Troy and I could see he was clueless.

In the elevator, Troy asked me, "What's going on?"

I answered in a low voice, "We'll talk about it later."

"What are you two talking about?" Bill asked.

"We were just wondering what's going on?" I asked.

"What do you think is going on?" Bill asked Troy, knowing I had figured it out already.

"I don't know," Troy answered, confused. "I am going to be real hungry by tonight."

Then Bill asked me the same question. I answered, "Well, I don't think you or Richard care if we eat, so you have other plans for us."

"Very smart, Timmy." What do you think they are?"

"You're going to pimp us out to someone else?"

"Well Timmy, you're right. But where did you get a word like that?"

"I heard it from Todd." Troy was looking at me, wondering how I'd figured this out. "Bill, are you going to be there?"

"No." Just you two"

"But you have nothing to worry about."

I had heard that before and had some of my worst nightmares come true. I knew that was all the information that Bill was giving out, so I dropped the subject.

Troy was starting to look really concerned, and I knew I had to distract him. He was the nicest kid in the group to me, and I didn't want him to worry when it wouldn't change anything. He hardly ever got mad at me and had never tried to cause trouble for me Troy was a kind hearted kid, so I made it my mission to get him through the hard times whatever we were about to go throw.

Bill gave the valet the ticket for the car, and soon we were off on our way. I started telling jokes in the car that my brother had told me, and I even had the men laughing. By the time we got to the mall, I could see that Troy was back to his old self.

Bill looked at me and said, "You're getting some new clothes today. I'm sick of the shit your mother buys for you, and I'm sick of seeing you in Tyler's hand-me-downs."

That was music to my ears. I totally scored, with five pairs of expensive jeans, ten really cool shirts, and a couple pairs of shoes and some socks. Troy got just as much as I did, and we both had a great time. The only difference was Troy could wear his new clothes whenever he wanted to. I was going to have to be smart and not raise any suspicion with my mom.

Bill looked at his watch and realized it was time to get back to the hotel. We were all carrying bags, and we had even made one trip to the car already. Back at the hotel, Bill told both of us to shower.

When I was done, I saw the clothes Bill had laid out for me, but I didn't see any underwear. I asked Bill, and he showed me the smallest thing I had ever seen. It was called a thong, and I had never seen men wear anything like that, let alone boys. I felt weird putting it on, but I knew better than to question him. I put on my other clothes and blow-dried my hair. Bill came in and checked me over. He told me I looked perfect and put some cologne on me.

We met Troy and Richard in the living room. Bill checked Troy over and was pleased and put some cologne on him. Bill had rented another hotel room and told us we would be going over there. He said, "This is a multimillion dollar deal. You do everything they ask and don't ask any questions." The way he said it put fear in both of us.

He opened the door and showed us which room we were to go to. We walked over and knocked on the door. To our surprise, it was opened up by a Japanese man. There were five men and one served as an interpreter. He motioned for us to go to the center of the room. He told us, "You are not to say a word. Just do as you are told. You will question nothing! Do you understand?"

We both nodded.

The lights were set on low, and he turned a lamp toward us to spotlight us.

The interpreter said to Troy, "You are the oldest, so you will be number one." He pointed to me. "You will be number two okay?"

They all sat down, and the interpreter began to give orders. He began by telling Troy to take off my shirt, and then I was to take off his. When we got as far as our underwear, all the men clapped in surprise at the thongs. We followed everything they said, and it was easy because it only involved Troy and I, and nothing was painful.

When that part was over, each of the men had a turn with one of us. It was disgusting because they were dirty, old men. It took a couple of hours until we were completely done.

The interpreter handed each of us five hundred dollars and said, "You both did very good. You tell Bill."

As we bent down to put our clothes back on, he pointed to the thongs and said, "Leave these. It will be our souvenir."

It didn't matter to us. We were just glad it was all over.

We turned to leave and one of the men said in broken English, "You two would do very well in Japan"

I knew this would be good news for Bill.

The man turns to the interpreter and spoke in Japanese. The interpreter walked us to the door and handed us some more money and said, "You thank Bill."

I smiled and nodded.

I knocked on our hotel room door, and Bill opened the door and asked right away, "How did it go?"

I handed him the envelope with his money in it, as I walked inside the room and said in my best Japanese accent, "It went very, very well."

Troy added, "They kept our underwear as souvenirs."

Richard and Bill laughed. Richard added, "I think that sealed our deal."

That's when I realized that Richard worked for Bill. I hadn't picked up on that before.

Bill said, "We'll see them tomorrow at the lunch meeting. Are you boy's hungry?"

"Yeah, we're starving," I said.

Troy and I ordered from room service.

After the food came, the men went back to their bedrooms. Troy and I took showers after we ate. We hung out in the living room area until we both fell asleep. It was after 11:00 a.m. before we woke up.

The men were gone, and a note told us to order room service. Troy called in our order and went to get dressed. The waiter came and set the food on the table and stood there looking at me. I realized I had to pay him and I went looking for my money from the night before.

He leaned over and handed me a piece of paper and said, "Just sign here."

"I've never done this before," I said.

The look on his faced seemed to say, "*Obviously*" He showed me the blank line for a tip, and I filled that in with "$20.00." That brought the first smile he had given me.

Troy and I sat around in our new clothes watching television. I asked him if he knew where we'd left our money last night because I couldn't find it. He reminded me that it was on the coffee table. I had looked, and it wasn't there. We didn't know where it had gone I figured Bill took it.

Bill and Richard came back a little after 1:00 p.m. They looked upset and disappointed.

Bill looked at both of us and said sternly, "You took money from them! You blew the deal!" Both of us looked terrified. "How could you do that?"

I started to explain with a shaky voice.

Then they both started laughing. "You guys were great. I wouldn't swear to it but you guys sealed the deal. They want to buy both of you tickets to Japan. Timmy, the head guy wants you to come back today."

"Why me" I asked disappointed.

I didn't like what had happened last night, and I thought it was all over.

"I guess you made quite an impression," Bill explained.

"What do I do?"

"You really have to ask? By now, you know the answer to that."

I knocked on the door, and the old man who had handed us the money was the one who opened it. He led me to the bedroom, and I was there for over an hour. He paid me again and told me in broken English that he wished he could take me back to Japan with him. All I could think is, *you old pervert.*

Back at the room, Bill asked, "Well, how do you think it went?"

"He's a pervert. How do you think it went?"

They all laughed, and that made me mad. I hadn't said it to be funny; it was the truth.

Troy asked, "How much did you make?"

I looked at him as if to say, *big mouth!* I don't know if he controlled his money, but I knew I didn't really control mine. Bill had the last say on my money.

Bill asked, "Yeah, Timmy, how much did you make?"

I pulled it out of my pocket and handed it to Bill. He counted it and said, "Wow! "You little slut" You must have been really good."

That pissed me off! I walked off to the bathroom and slammed the door. I took off my clothes and threw away the underwear, like it was a reminder of all that the lifestyle had taken from me. I got in the shower and had it as hot as I could handle it, hoping to wash away all I had been through in the last two days. The door opened and Bill walked in. I knew I had locked it, I don't know how he got in. The shower glass door was clear, and we could see each other.

"What's wrong?" Bill asked me.

"It's just . . . Never mind."

"What is it, Timmy? You can tell me."

"No I can't. You'll just get mad."

"No I won't. Tell me."

"You don't do anything with me. I do what you want and go where you want to go. You're proud of me when it's convenient and ashamed of me all the other times."

"No I'm not."

"Yes, you are! Why is my room hidden downstairs in the locker room? You have empty bedrooms upstairs that no one is using. You don't take me anywhere unless you need me to do something for you." I turned off the shower and wrapped a towel around me. "You make me do things I don't want to do. Then you take my money and laugh at me, calling me a slut." I stood there staring at him waiting for him to yell at me or intimidate me into going back on everything I'd finally had the guts to say to his face. I wasn't used to be treating like this because Brian had been my only experience. He had made me feel special, like a son, most of the time.

He looked me in the eye and surprised the hell out of me. "You're right. I'm sorry. I will change that." Then he walked out of the room.

Cool, I thought. Then I got dressed and walked into the living room and found the luggage had already been taken downstairs.

In the car, everyone was in a good mood. Bill wasn't even mad at me. We stopped at a really expensive steak house. Bill told us to order anything we wanted. Troy knew right away what he wanted, but I still wasn't used to ordering for myself. Bill saw that I was having trouble and ordered me the same thing he was having.

While we were waiting for the food, Bill said, "You still have the rest of the week off."

I nodded at him. He had already told me what I needed to accomplish this week, and I didn't want to think about it. I was going to have to start remaking the movies with Rick and Todd.

Then he surprised me and asked, "What do you want to do tomorrow?"

"Really" I would like to go to Palm Springs?"

"Why Palm Springs?"

"Because you guys are always talking about your trips there, and I've never been there."

"Okay, Timmy, that's where we will go—just you and me."

"Really"

"Yes."

"That's cool!"

On the ride back to Bill's house, Troy and I were joking and laughing. Troy got serious for a moment and asked me, "Timmy, will you go out with me?"

I thought he meant there was something special he wanted to do so I said, "Sure."

He smiled and we went back to playing around.

Bill's Turn around

As soon as we got to Bill's house, we helped load up Richard's car with all the shopping bags and luggage. Troy walked over to tell me good-bye. He leaned over and gave me a French kiss. This totally shocked me!

I'd seen other people—like Brian and Roger and even some of the other men—French-kiss. One time in a movie, they wanted Carlos and I to do that. But it looked so fake that they dropped it. I pushed him away from me, and he thought this was fun, so he laughed and headed to the car.

I spit on the lawn Bill looked at me and asked, "What in the hell is that all about?"

"You got me!" He just French-kissed me"

"Why?"

"I think he was just screwing around."

We walked into the house. Carrying all my new clothes, I headed for my room.

"Where are you going?" Bill asked.

"I'm just going to put my new clothes up."

"Where"

I gave him a weird look and said, "In my room."

He raised his voice and said, "That's not your room anymore."

Bill was not a man you wanted to piss off, and I got scared.

Then he smiled and said, "Let me show you to your new room."

I followed him upstairs and two doors down from Tyler's room. I remembered being in here before, and I was having trouble comprehending all this. Bill wasted no time changing how he treated me, and I was in shock because of it.

"Wow! You're going to give me this room?"

Bill had a big smile. He was enjoying my pure enthusiasm. "Yes!"

"Holy shit"

The room had white carpet and a huge bed. A bearskin rug sat next to a couch in front of a fireplace. There was a huge bathroom that put what my parents had to shame.

"Well, what do you think?" Bill asked.

"It's great!" I turned and gave him a big hug. I couldn't believe my good fortune. Bill really did care; he just hadn't realized that he wasn't showing it.

"We can fix this up anyway you want it. I'll have my decorator help you with some ideas."

"Really"

"Sure, Timmy, whatever makes you happy." I knew I couldn't spend as much time as I wanted to in that room, but it felt great to know that it was there. I made sure Bill knew I was sincerely grateful for the room.

On the way back to my house, we talked about our plans for tomorrow. Bill would pick me up at 7:00 a.m. because it was a two-hour drive.

I walked up to the door and listened, and I heard music. That was odd because dad's truck was gone. I walked in and could smell dinner cooking. I went by Tommy's room. It was empty, so I headed for the kitchen. Mom was moving to the music while she cooked.

She turned to me and said, "Good, you're home."

"Hi, Mom" How are you doing?"

"Great! Come over here and give me a kiss."

I walked over to her and she bent down for a kiss and said, "I love you, Timmy."

"Love you too, Mom."

These were the times that I wished filled my memory of her. This is what I thought most kids got to have at home. It was like she was two different people, and every now and then, I got a glimpse of what could have been.

"What's for dinner?"

"Your favorite—, ham, black-eyed peas, corn bread, and cooked carrots."

I don't know what kid she was thinking about, but the only thing that would be easy for me to swallow would be the ham.

"Where is everybody?"

"Your dad is out of town, and Tommy is staying at a friend's house."

I didn't want to get in trouble tonight, and since she was in a good mood, I didn't want to hurt her feelings either. So I grabbed a small plastic bag and put it in my lap. I ate what I could and slipped the other stuff in the bag. I used every opportunity to distract her, and it worked. After dinner, I put the bag in the outside trash can and pushed it down to the middle.

She washed the dishes, and I dried and put them away. We both got ready for bed, and she asked if I wanted to watch TV with her. We stayed up late, and she cuddled with me on the couch. I wished it could be like this all the time, but I knew better.

After she went to bed, I thought to myself that she doesn't even know the real me. Hell, I don't even know myself. I had gone from victim to willing participant like a trained animal, and now I found myself still doing whatever the guys in the group asked of me. It seemed there wasn't anything I wouldn't do for love or attention, or even for money. Thinking about it made me sick to my stomach. I had gone too far and done unspeakable things in the last couple of years, and they held proof of all of it in pictures and movies. I couldn't see any way out this time.

I was thinking way too much this late at night, and Bill was coming by early in the morning to pick me up. I went to my bedroom and set the alarm and did my best to go right to sleep.

I must have hit the snooze button because, when I looked at the clock, I only had ten minutes to get ready and meet Bill two blocks away. Bill was a stickler for being on time, and I ended up being five minutes late. Because this was a fun day he didn't seem to mind. He brought his black Porsche instead of the Mercedes because he knew I loved riding with the top down. I knew that, when we got to the desert, we would have to put the top up because it would be too hot and dusty.

"So, Timmy, you really want to go to Palm Springs?"

"Yeah, it's hot there and we can swim and lay out."

"True."

"I want to go to the place Brian and Roger are always talking about."

"Okay, but things don't liven up until it gets dark. It's so hot during the day that people stay inside."

"Oh, so we'll have the pool all to ourselves then?"

"Well, I think you will give a reason for them to come out."

I had no idea what he meant by that, and we started talking about other things. When we reached our destination, I wasn't nearly as impressed as I thought I would be. I expected a high-rise hotel with maybe a tropical setting. Instead I saw a two story apartment complex with colored rock used as decorations.

We walked to the middle where the pool was and it was even less impressive than I had hoped for. Bill's pool was much fancier than this one. I asked Bill, "Is this a hotel?"

"No, it's an elite apartment complex. All the guests are handpicked."

"Why?"

"You'll see."

We walked past the pool and to a single-story building, Jerry's Bar and Grill. There was a sign on the door. "You're welcome, but your clothes aren't." And under it was another saying, "Boys Will Be Boys Nudist Colony."

I looked at Bill surprised as hell, and he laughed and said, "You wanted to come here."

Three men sat at the bar naked, smoking and drinking. It was only 9:00 a.m., and I couldn't believe what I was seeing. I was used to this happening at the parties but never in any other situation. Two of the guys looked really good, but the third—well, some people were just made for clothes.

The man who ran the bar came out from the back and said, "Bob, I was surprised to get your call last night." I was thinking that now Bill had a third name. I was too young to know that Robert and Bob meant the same thing. "This must be Timmy."

"Yes, it is," Bill replied.

"You are quite the star around here. But you do look different with your clothes on."

My mouth dropped open now, it was all coming together. This was a gay nudist place. I would never have asked to come if I had known this is a community of gay pedophiles.

"Are you guy's hungry?"

Bill looked at me, and I nodded yes. I was starving because I had thrown away most of my dinner last night.

"Okay then," the man said and headed to the back to cook us up something.

One of the men at the bar looked at us and pointed to another sign that read "Changing Room "Bill looked at me and asked, "Are you ready?"

I didn't even answer. I just followed him.

When we got inside, I asked, "Why didn't you tell me?"

"Now what fun would that have been? Plus, you would have changed your mind."

"Yeah, I would have. I had no idea. Have those guys seen some of our movies?"

"Yeah, Timmy, you have made movie night around here pretty memorable," he answered as he started to undress. "Your turn," he said as he puts his clothes in a locker.

"They'll all be staring at us."

"No not at us but at you" Don't worry. Nothing will happen to you here."

"Promise"

"I promise. No one here can afford you," he answered with a laugh. "I'll be waiting for you."

"Wait, Bill, please, don't leave me." I hurried up and undressed and shoved my clothes in a locker. There was no way I wanted to walk out there alone.

Before he opened the door, he asked me, "Are you ready?"

"I guess if I have to."

"Yes, you have to. We've come this far. We're not going back just yet."

I followed Bill to a table, not looking at anyone. I was so embarrassed I didn't know what to do. It wasn't until I sat down that I realized the table at least covered me for now. By then, I could finally look up at everyone. Two of the men nodded their approval at me, and I wanted to be anywhere else but here.

The bartender brought our food out and sat and talked with Bill as we ate. When I finished eating, Bill told me I could go swimming and he would join me in a little while. It was a short walk, but I was conscious of every step I had to take. Nobody was around the pool, but it felt like I was being watched by everyone behind their apartment doors. I quickly jumped in, glad that it offered some semblance of coverage. I was shocked to find out how warm the pool was. It wasn't as hot as a Jacuzzi, but it was a lot warmer than any other pool I had ever been in. I guessed the sun kept the temperature high all the time.

About fifteen minutes later, Bill jumped in the pool. He threw a handful of change in the deep end for me to dive and get it. We did this a couple of times. It was getting boring. But I was amazed that Bill was playing with me. That was great! I brought up the last coin and realized that he thought this game would tire me out. I was going too be eleven years old; I was just getting started.

I knew Bill needed some help from me, so I suggested, "Bill, let's race."

He smiled easily and agreed, and we went to the shallow end first. With all the time I spend in a pool, I had been racing against older, stronger people like Carlos for a while, and I was getting real good. I hoped I wouldn't beat him too badly. I said, "Go" and swam as fast as I could.

Even with a good push off, Bill beat me by a longshot. I thought this was just a fluke and challenged him to another race. I had a great start, but just like last time, he beat me with time to spare. He really surprised me with his speed. My next try was different. I got to dive in, and I just knew that would give me the speed I needed. By this time, I forgot to be self-conscious when I was outside the pool. But I did notice that there were about five guys now at the pool watching us race.

After Bill won that race, I was feeling truly defeated.

Bill said, "What, Timmy, you don't want to try again?"

"Nope you win"

"How about I will swim backwards and you can dive in with a head start?"

I knew these were the best conditions I would ever get, so I tried one more time. I jumped in as far as I could and swam with all my strength, and to my amazement, Bill still passed me.

He had won pretty easily, but he was getting out of breath from racing me. He leaned against the side in the deep end and stayed there to relax. I couldn't stand up there, so I held onto his neck making him hold both of us up. He did this easily.

I looked him in the eye and asked, "Tell me?"

"Tell you what?"

"Were you state champion or something in college?"

He laughed, "As a matter of fact, I was runner up."

"I knew it!"

Then we both laughed.

I looked around, and some of the guys who had been lying out were now in the shallow end. There were a few more guys coming through the gate to the pool.

So much for having it to ourselves, I thought.

Bill let go of the side and told me to get on his back. He swam to the other end. "You wore me out," he said. "I am going to lie out for a while." Bill turned to the group of men and said, "Guys, this is Timmy."

I didn't know why he did that. It actually made me kind of nervous.

They introduced themselves, and Barry said to me, "Ron told us you're the kid from the movie we saw awhile back. He's right, isn't he?"

I just looked at him and swam away. I heard the other guys call him an asshole. I was holding onto the ledge in the deep end when

Barry swam over to apologize to me. "I'm sorry. I didn't mean to embarrass you."

I just looked at him and asked, "Which one did you see?"

"Actually, I've seen two. One was *Child Slave* and the other was *Hard Core Kid.*"

Shit, I thought, *they actually named them.* I had no idea which ones he was talking about.

Barry could tell I was confused and asked, "You don't know which ones I am talking about, do you?"

"No."

"How many have you done?"

I just looked at him and replied, "Too many, I guess."

I wanted to change the subject, and Barry got the hint when I swam away. He followed me back to the other side. One of the guys had gotten the volleyball and asked me if I wanted to play. It was funny to me that this group of gay guys did the same stuff we did at the parties. I had a feeling I was the only reason they were down at the pool during the heat of the day. The water had become so warm it didn't even really cool you off. I told him that I wasn't that good, but nobody seemed to care.

They divided up into two teams. About half of these guys were in decent shape, and the other half needed to diet. But I have to give it to them; they played to win. When we played at the parties, the guys didn't care if we missed the ball or lost a game. They let me get in a few hits, but when our team started winning, they would spike it toward me to gain some points.

Someone hit the ball out of the water and I looked around and saw Bill talking to the biggest bodybuilder I had ever laid eyes on. This guy's muscles had muscles. He was about five foot nine or so, and he had washboard abs and a lot of definition. He had to be a pro bodybuilder.

Bill walked to the side of the pool and said to me, "Timmy, I want you to meet someone."

I swam over to the edge and got out of the water.

"This is Phil."

"Hi."

"Hi, Timmy" It's really nice to meet you. When I found out you were here today, I just had to come meet you."

I smiled. "You came out to meet me?"

"Yeah"

I about fell over.

Bill said, "You can go back to the game now."

We started a new game, and one of my teammates told me if the other team spiked it toward me, he would get it. This helped a lot, and we got down to the game-winning point. Barry spiked the ball hard and fast I couldn't get out of the way. It hit me hard in the face and knocked me out cold. I woke up on the side of the pool with Bill putting ice on my nose and lips.

I started to cry from the pain even though I didn't want to.

"Calm down, Timmy," Bill said. "You're going to be all right."

Everyone was standing around me staring, and that made me feel even more uncomfortable.

Bill said, "He'll be all right."

The guys get back in the pool.

Barry apologized, and Bill accepted the apology for me. I felt like the guy had tried to kill me, so I wasn't going to accept it. The other guys called him an asshole for the second time.

Bill and Phil helped me to my feet but everything started to spin. They laid me down again but the ground was too hot.

"It's burning my back," I told Bill.

He carried me to the Bar and Grill and laid me on the cool floor and covered me with a towel. I laid there for about ten or fifteen minutes, and when I got up, I felt a lot better.

I told Bill I had to go to the bathroom, and I looked in the mirror and was shocked at how much damage it had done. My lips and nose were swollen.

Bill said, "You're going to have two black eyes out of this."

"What will I tell my parents?

"Tell them the truth—you got hit in the face with a ball. Just don't tell them you were in Palm Springs when it happened."

The guys from the pool were now at the bar waiting to see if I was all right. Bill told them again that I was fine. Barry apologized again, and I accepted this time. They asked if I wanted to go back in the pool, but Bill told them I'd had enough for today.

"What do you want to do?" Bill asked me.

"I want to lie down for a while. My head hurts."

"I bet it does. I'll get you something for your headache, and you can go get dressed."

Bill came back with some Tylenol, and he got ready to go too. He said good-bye to everyone, but he took Phil aside and gave him some money and said, "I'll see you tomorrow."

We went back to the Porsche and tried to ride with the top down, but it was just too hot. Bill put the top back on and turned on the air conditioner.

"It's hotter than hell here. Why do people live here?"

"I have no idea. I could never do it."

"Me neither."

"What do you want to do for the rest of the day?"

"What is there to do around here?"

"Not much for someone your age."

"Let's just go home."

"How does your head feel?"

"It still hurts."

"Put your seat back and close your eyes."

I fell right to sleep and didn't wake up until we pulled into the driveway. It was still early, and I was still feeling tired.

Bill said, "If you're still tired, then go lay down for a while."

Just what I wanted—an excuse to go lay down on that huge bed in my new room.

A couple of hours later, Tyler came in and woke me up. "Dad says it's time to get up."

I moaned, "No, Tyler, I don't want to get up yet. I was having the perfect dream."

"Well Dad wants to take us out to eat. He wants you to call your parents and ask if you can spend the night I rolled away from him, wishing he would disappear for just a little while longer. He moved towards me shaking my shoulder. I rolled on my back, and he looked shocked. "What happened to your face?"

"I got hit in the face with a stupid volleyball"

"Bullshit! It looks more like you got hit with a truck."

"Ask your dad if you don't believe me."

"Well get up. We are going out."

I rolled out of bed. My headache was still there, but I really did feel rested. I was already dressed, but I went into my new huge bathroom and fixed my hair and brushed my teeth. Tyler left to go get ready. I ran down the stairs. Bill was getting impatient waiting for us.

"How do you feel?"

"Good" I lied.

"Glad to hear it. But you sure don't look any better."

I agreed with him, having seen myself in the bathroom mirror.

"Call home and ask if you can spend the night."

I went into Bill's office to use the phone. Mom answered the phone, and she was in a good mood. She told me I could stay and didn't even ask any questions. When I returned, I told Bill I could stay, and by then, Tyler was finally ready.

We went in the Mercedes, and Bill drove us to a steakhouse that sat high on a hill and overlooked the city. I was surprised to see that Rick, Todd, Richard, and Troy were already there waiting for us.

Troy asked right away what had happened to my face, and I was already tired of explaining it, even though I knew I had only started telling the people in our group that I'd have to tell.

Rick told Bill, "There's an hour's wait tonight."

Bill replied, "Really. I'll be right back."

Bill asked the host to get the manager, and five minutes later, we were sitting at a table next to a large window with a great view of the city. I sat with Troy on one side and Tyler on the other. Since Tyler didn't know everything that went on, Troy and I had to be careful of our conversation.

I overheard Bill talking about Phil and listened to what they were saying

Todd asked, "Is Phil still big?"

"Bigger than ever," Bill answered. "He's coming to the studio to be in one of our films."

Todd was amazed and said, "I must have asked him a hundred times, and he always turned me down. He said no amount of money could change his mind."

"Well, he's seen a couple of the movies and has finally changed his mind. I also told him that his identity would never be revealed. But I think the thing that really sold him was that he met Timmy. His attitude changed right after that."

The men turned and looked at me.

Todd asked, "What about his face?"

Bill replied, "It will only make it more realistic."

They all thought about it and agreed.

Troy turned to me and asked, "Whose Phil?"

I explained, "He's a bodybuilder and the biggest guy I've ever seen."

"Wow, it sucks to be you."

Tyler heard that and laughed.

"What do you mean?" I asked.

"I hope he doesn't make you a new asshole," Troy replied.

Bill overheard this and said sternly, "You watch your mouth!"

Troy nodded his head in understanding.

The food came out, and the talk quieted some while we enjoyed a good meal. When Troy got done eating, he reached under the table and took my hand. No one else could see this, and even though it was a little weird, all my experiences with this group were weird. The boys in the group shared a strange closeness, partly because of the secrecy that we had to live in.

After dinner was over, the men walked over to Richard's car and kept talking while we kids went to Bill's car. Troy said, "I'm going to try to come over with Richard tomorrow."

"Don't you have school?" I asked.

"Yeah, but I really want to meet Phil," Troy explained.

"What are you guys talking about?" Tyler finally asked. Even with all the talk at dinner, Tyler had not put it together yet.

Troy explained, "They are making another movie tomorrow."

"Really" So that's what you guys were talking about," Tyler said. "I've met Phil. I'd like to be there too."

I was thinking, great; *invite the whole neighborhood, like it isn't hard enough just to get through a day like that.* I had mixed feelings. A part of me didn't even want to be there, let alone participate. Yet the part that had become hardened to this side of my life was proud that I was the one Phil had picked, and I liked being the center of attention.

Troy put his arm around me, and I put my arm across his shoulders while we continued to talk to Tyler.

Richard called for Troy, and he turned to me and said, "I love you," and kissed me on the lips before running to the car.

I was shocked. I loved him too, but not in that way.

"What was that all about?" Tyler asked in amazement.

I answered just as shocked, "Hell, Tyler, I have no idea!"

We got in the car with Bill, and Tyler couldn't wait to tell his dad what had just happened with Troy. I reached over to hit him, hoping he would shut up.

Bill's answer to the situation was, "That's what guys do when they are going out?"

My mouth dropped open, and I said, "Oh shit! That's why he kissed me the other day. I thought he was just joking, and I went along with it. I didn't know he was serious. I hated it when he kissed me!"

"Why?" Bill asked laughing.

"Because it's gross"

"What's gross?" Bill asked, pushing me to say it out loud.

"French-kissing"

"After what you two have done, Bill said I wouldn't think a kiss would freak you out. You are one weird kid, Timmy "I just sat there, wanting to defend myself but finding it hard to explain. He was right about part of it. But I felt like everything I had done and experienced was because the group had made me or blackmailed me, even though I had become used to it. These weren't things I would ever choose to do on my own. These things never touched the other part of my life.

"What's wrong, Timmy?" Bill asked after a few minutes of silence.

"Nothing"

Then Tyler changed the subject and asked his dad, "Can I stay home tomorrow and watch them film the movie?"

"Absolutely not"

"Why?"

"Because you're going to the beach house with your friends from school"

Tyler was mad, but he dropped it.

Back at the house, I was wide awake because of the naps I had taken. Bill told us to shower and get ready for bed. I went to my new room and decided to soak in the bathtub before going to bed. I was trying to decide what to do about Troy because he really was a good friend and had a heart of gold. I didn't want to hurt his feelings but I sure wasn't comfortable with our new friendship. I went under the water and held my breath for as long as I could. I liked seeing how high I could count. I went under again, and suddenly I didn't feel like I was alone anymore. I came up out of the water kind of fast and wiped my eyes to see what had made me uneasy.

"Tyler, you scared me," I said, startled at his presence. I thought I had locked the door.

"Sorry, I knocked on the door, but you didn't answer, so I came in," he explained.

I grabbed a towel and wrapped it around me. He was sitting on the edge of the tub, and I thought he had his shirt off. But I quickly realized that he was naked. It wasn't that long ago that he would have been too embarrassed to do that.

He stood up and grabbed the corner of my towel and said, "You won't need that." As he walked toward me, I backed up. He kept pushing until my back hit the wall. I could tell by the look in his eye that he liked having this control. I went under his arm, headed for the bedroom, and he grabbed my arm and swung me around. I was headed for the fireplace, which was now lit, and kept my footing so I only hit the mantel. He apologized profusely, but I knew this wouldn't stop him from his original plan.

For some reason, I thought this room would, or could, be a safe haven for me. It made me mad that I had no choice in these kinds of matters. I knew tomorrow would be hard for me, and I wanted the night off. But it was easier to just get it over with and go to bed than to fight.

The Perfect Body

After Tyler left, I crawled right into bed. The fireplace was going strong and making the room nice and warm. It wasn't long before I fell asleep. If I had known how bad my nightmares were going to be, I would have just stayed awake all night.

I woke to Bill shaking me and yelling, "Timmy, stop" Wake up!"

I opened my eyes and knew that I had been screaming.

Bill picked me up, and feeling his strength helped some of the demons in my mind flee. He carried me to his room, and I was exhausted enough to fall back to sleep, hoping and praying for no more nightmares.

When I woke up and looked around, I remembered what had happened last night.

Bill was getting dressed and saw me move around and said, "Good morning."

I returned the greeting, sounding a little groggy.

Bill sat down next to me and said, "You had a nightmare last night. Do you remember what it was about?"

I shook my head no, lying to him, unsure how to explain all the horrible images that had gone through my mind.

"Timmy, you can't fall asleep with the fireplace on. Do you understand?"

"Yes, sir" I nodded solemnly.

"What do your parents do when you have nightmares?"

"They don't know about them."

"Timmy, you were screaming and crying in your sleep. How could they not hear you?"

"Maybe it's never happened before?"

"Yeah, right"

"Bill, where are you going?"

"I have to be in the office today. I have some meetings and won't be home until tonight."

"So, we aren't doing the movies today?"

"Yes, we are. I just won't be here."

"Bill, please!"

"Please what?"

"Don't leave me today. My nightmares were about the movie today, and I'm really scared. Rick and Todd were out of control and Phil was doing horrible things to me." I hadn't been afraid of Phil when I met him, but after last night I was scared to death.

"Timmy, it was just a bad dream, not reality."

"I just feel better when you are there."

"Why?"

"Because it makes everyone behave."

He laughed out loud. "Really" Will everyone is already here and you need to shower and get ready. I promise everyone will behave." He lifted my chin so that I was looking him in the eye and said, "Do you understand?"

"Yes."

Then he kissed the top of my head and said good-bye.

Resigned to my immediate future, I walked back to my bedroom and got ready. While I was in the shower, Anna had made my bed and put my clean clothes away. It made me laugh because, in my wildest dreams, my own mother would never do that for me. I got dressed and realized how ironic it was because I wouldn't stay that way long. I looked in the mirror to fix my hair and saw that I was bruised under my eyes and my lip was a little swollen.

I walked down the stairs and figured I had to get this over with sooner or later. I heard several conversations and recognized most of the voices. Anna was in the kitchen cooking for the whole group. Rick, Todd, Craig, Phil, Richard, and Troy were there.

As I walked in, Phil had his back to me, and it was literally the biggest back I had ever seen. His back was huge and V-shaped; they tapered down to a small waist. I walked over to where Troy was sitting. He was hanging on every word that Phil was saying.

Phil looked up to see me and said, "Wow, Timmy, that ball did a number on you."

"Hi, Phil, I can't believe you're here."

He was sitting with his elbows on the table, and I couldn't believe how huge his arms were.

He looked at Troy and me and said, "I can't believe I'm here either."

Everyone filled their plates and started talking over the details of the day.

Anna fixed my plate and set it down in front of me. She lifted my chin up and asked, "What happened?"

"I got hit in the face with "volleyball""

She just looked at me like she didn't believe me and patted me on the head.

"If that will be all, then I will excuse myself," Anna announced.

Everyone thanked her, and she walked out to start on her other duties.

Todd was already walking toward me, and he took my plate of food. I grabbed a piece of bacon before he could stop me. "You can eat later."

I swallowed the bacon, grateful for even that little bit. What happened to the good old days when they fed you when you were hungry?

Phil looked surprised, so Troy explained it to him. While they were talking, Troy slipped me another piece of bacon under the table. Phil saw this and smiled. Looking at Phil reminded me of when I used to work out with Brian. I used to think Brian had muscles, but being this close to Phil and realizing just how huge he was opened up a whole new world for me.

Rick came over and told Troy to move so he could go over the first scene with both of us. I flashed back to the first time we did this and had goose bumps. I pushed away the memories so I could get through the day. We went to the studio, and the lights were already on, heating up the room unfortunately. The rack was sitting on a small stage, and whips, chains, and straps hung from the wall. A bar with hand straps hung from a cable hooked to a wench. This was all done to look like a dungeon.

They took Phil to the changing room so he could get dressed in a leather outfit. The other guys were all getting the cameras and equipment ready.

Troy was standing next to me and whispered, "I wish I was you."

I looked at him totally shocked. I wished he was me too, but wishing wasn't going to change anything.

Phil came walking out wearing a black leather Speedo and a leather vest. His chest was so huge the vest barely fit him. He had on a Zorro mask that did nothing to hide his real identity. He walked over to us and asked nervously, "What do we do now?"

I shrugged my shoulders and said, "Just wait until they are ready."

Todd yelled, "Everyone, take your places"

Craig shot Todd a look that said he wasn't the one in charge.

"Sorry, Craig" That must have been hard for Todd because he was one of the founders of this sick production company.

The first scene started, and Phil grabbed my arms and pushed me to the steps of the stage. He picked me up and shoved my back against the rack. Unfortunately, Phil didn't know his own strength. But after all I had been through; I knew when to shut up.

To my relief, Craig said, "Cut. Remember, Phil, we are only acting. We really don't want to hurt anyone. Timmy, come with me."

Craig took me into the dressing room and added some makeup to enhance the bruises under my eyes. I didn't like wearing makeup and told him. He told me to quit whining and turned me to the mirror. I could see that he'd done a really good job. Then he took scissors and made a couple of cuts in my shirt. "Perfect," he said.

Craig marched me out of the room, and everyone fell silent. It was quite the transformation.

Todd smiled and said, "That's perfect!"

The scene started over again. Phil used a lighter touch, and I filled in the rest with my acting abilities. Having someone so large next to my small frame was going to add to the intensity of the moment. The guys were looking pleased with the effect. Phil was not used to the kinds of scenes we had to do, and we had to start over many times. By the time they called it a day, I had spent over five hours on that damn rack.

Phil undid the straps and helped me off the rack, and I fell to the floor and couldn't get up. Phil panicked thinking that he had really hurt me. I explained that my legs had been asleep for a long time.

When the blood returned to my legs and I could stand, Troy and I took off for the pool. The water always felt refreshing and cleansing. I needed that because I always felt dirty afterward. Eventually I could put it out of my mind, but first I had to get it off my body.

Troy was the first to speak. He had been quiet all day. "Timmy, you did great today."

"I really didn't do anything but lay on that stupid rack all day."

He laughed, "Yeah, but just wait until you see how great it turned out."

We stayed in the pool about an hour before they called us in. Everyone was waiting for us in the TV room. I hated this part. It was bad enough being in one of their sick movies, but having to watch myself was the absolute worse. Bill and Tyler were home, and everyone was just waiting for us.

Craig said, "Can't wait to get started. The finished product will look a lot better, but we got some great footage today."

I was amazed at how I looked on screen this time. I was pale and small with a battered face. I had sweat running down my head and face onto my body. It was so real it was scary. Everyone else sat in stunned silence.

When Craig shut it off he asked, "What do you think?"

Todd broke the silence and said, "Wow! That was great!"

Everyone started clapping and congratulating us. I wanted to throw up watching it seem to be worse for me than actually acting in one. I knew I had sealed my fate for making more movies, and that was utterly discouraging. Bill walked over to check on me, and I said, "I'm really hungry. I haven't eaten all day." Earlier it had been more important to get cleaned off then to eat.

Tyler walked over. "I'll get you something to eat," he said.

Troy came with us to the kitchen, and we raided the refrigerator.

I went home later that evening. I wore a baseball cap low on my head to cover my black eyes. Dad was out of town again, and Mom was in bed with a headache again. She got up a couple of hours later and fixed grilled cheese and soup for us. She freaked out when she saw my black eyes and asked, "Timmy, what happened to you?"

""volleyball hit me in the face," I said and she felt satisfied and let it go.

She didn't ask any more questions, just took some more Valium and went back to bed. She and Dad were having marriage problems. Dad was drinking more when he was at home. But lately he worked out of town a lot.

The next day I rode my bike to Bill's. I ride my bike most days so I could stop and get something to eat. It was easier to handle a long day in the torture room when you at least started with food in your system.

They wanted me early on most morning, but I accidentally overslept. I was supposed to be there at 8:00 but didn't arrive until 9:30. Todd was pissed off at me, but that wasn't new in our relationship.

I was surprised to see Joey there and even more surprised when Brian wasn't there with him. Joey was talking to Troy, and it looked like they had both been crying. I asked them what was wrong, and they both shrugged it off.

Todd walked over and said, "They are both acting like babies. Troy is crying because he can't be in the movie, and Joey is crying because he is going to be in the movie."

I answered, "That's an easy fix. Let Troy take Joey's place." This was the wrong thing to say to Todd.

"Who the hell do you think you are?" You little son of a bitch! He slapped my face so hard that I fell to the ground.

I was shocked at how fast he had gone off on me and was barely able to holding back my tears.

Roger heard the commotion and walked in to find me sitting on the floor holding my face. The other adults had walked in but didn't do a thing. Roger walked right up to Todd and punched him, knocking him to the floor. Todd got off the floor as quickly as he could and the other guys finally stepped in and stopped the fight. Rick and Todd were yelling and cussing at each other. It reminded me of a family reunion on my mom's side.

Bill came from his office after hearing all the noise and yelled, "That's enough!" Everyone stopped. He walked over to me and reached out a hand. I grabbed it and got off the floor. He turned to the other kids and said, "Go check out Timmy's new room." We all ran out of the room, glad to be gone and even gladder that Bill wasn't going to yell at us.

We all walked into my room. Troy and Joey were shocked at how huge it was. They really liked the decorations, and thought it looked really cool but it didn't take long for our mood to change, we all just had a traumatic experience. Joey was still very upset about the movie, and I was pissed at Todd for hitting me.

Troy asked, "What the hell was that all about?"

I commented, "Todd is such an asshole!"

We were all setting on the couch Joey drops his head between his knees and mumbled "I don't want to be here." Then he reached into his pocket and pulled out a bag with some pills in it.

I quickly grabbed the bag out of his hand. Troy was surprised and had no idea what was happening.

"Joey, where the hell do you get this stuff?" I asked on my way to the bathroom to flush them down the toilet.

Joey rushed after me to stop me and said, "I stole them from my dad. Don't flush them. I have enough for all of us."

"Is that the same stuff that you gave me last time?"

He nodded and started crying. I put my arm around him and led him back to the couch. "Joey, those pills don't make it any easier; they just screw you up."

"That's what I want!"

"No you don't! They make you think stuff happened that really didn't. I still have nightmares from that night."

Troy finally pieced it all together, and before he could speak, Bill opened up the bedroom door. Seeing Joey still crying and upset, he asked exasperated, "Now what's wrong?"

"Joey is upset, and I am taking care of it."

Bill looks at me, concerned and proud at the same time, "Okay, time out "You boys just relax. We are taking the day off. You guys decide what you want to do today. Timmy, get Joey settled down and come back downstairs. Troy, come with me." He walked back downstairs.

"Joey, if we would have taken those pills, we would all be wasted right now and the memories wouldn't be true."

"What do you mean?"

I told him the memories the drug had left me with—the crazy dream of being tied down and raped by all the men in the room, even his own dad.

Joey looked at me with a deadpan face and said, "Yeah, I know, I was there."

"Well what happened?"

"Pretty much everything you think happened."

I was in complete shock and denial.

He continued, "That's why I gave you the pill." Then he got off the couch and walked out the door.

I sat there too stunned to move. How could he be so coldhearted?

Then he came back to the doorway and said, "Just kidding!" He ran down the stairs. I jumped off the couch, feeling relief from his answer and ready to wrestle him to the ground.

As we all stood before Bill, he asked, "So what do you boys want to do?"

We all agreed on going to the park and playing flag football. We walked out and started loading up in different cars, and I headed to Bill's car. I opened the door and he said, "You go ride with Rick and Todd."

I looked more closely at him, hoping he was kidding. He wasn't.

"Bill, Todd hates me!"

"That's ridiculous. He wants to apologize to you. Now go!"

Joey and Troy were getting in Bill's backseat because they wanted to ride with me. "Where are you going?" Troy asked.

"I have to ride with Todd."

They both gave me a look of sympathy, and Troy replied, "Better you than me."

Joey said, "Good luck." Then they both laughed.

It was only a short ride to the park, and I got in the car acting like nothing was wrong. Todd seemed uncomfortable; he never liked apologizing. I'm sure he felt himself to be above apologizing to a kid. He was a man who other adults turned to and looked up to him a person that made life and death decisions for others. The general public saw the side of him that kept the Hippocratic Oath. I, unfortunately, saw the sick and demented side of him and felt him completely capable of killing me if he could get away with it.

Todd cleared his throat and said in a low, monotone voice, "Timmy, I'm sorry. I didn't mean to hit you."

That was the lamest apology yet. If I wasn't so scared of him, I would have told him to shove it. But I had no choice and no idea when I would be at his mercy again. "No problem," I replied, glad that this uncomfortable moment was over.

There was a deafening silence for a few moments, and Rick spoke up, "So, it's your birthday coming up. You're goanna be eleven right?"

"Yeah, that's right." Actually, I had forgotten that my birthday was almost here.

"You know there is going to be a big party for you. What do you want?"

"I really want motocross."

Todd asks, "You want another bike?"

"No. I want a motorcycle."

"Really," Todd answered, "that's a lot of money."

"I've got most of it."

Rick added, "I've still got some of your money at my house."

I knew that it was over nine hundred dollars. I hadn't forgotten about that. I just didn't know if I would ever see it again.

Todd, being the expected pessimist, said, "You know you can't take a gift like that home."

"I can't take any of my gifts home anyway."

This shut Todd up, and we arrived at the park a few minutes later.

We met the others, and Bill told Troy and me that we would be team captains. I knew Troy would pick the guys he wanted to suck up to in hopes of getting in a movie. I, on the other hand, picked the most athletic guys because I wanted to win.

We won the first couple of games by a landslide. Bill decided we needed to even out the teams to make it more fun. I was proud of myself for having done so well. Someone had called the other guys in the group and told them where we were. As the men showed up, they would join a team, and the games kept getting better and better.

At around 2:00, some of the guys went to the store and bought what we needed to barbecue at the park. It had been a very long time since I'd had this much fun with the guys.

Bill was sitting across from me, and Joey and Troy were on each side of me. The men wanted to sit at Bill's table, so it was really full.

Bill asked us boys, "Are you having fun?"

Joey and Troy answered, "Yeah!"

I looked at Bill and smiled broadly and said, 'The best"

Rick was next to Bill and asked, "Did you ask Timmy what he wants for his birthday?"

I could tell by the expression that Bill had forgotten and was working at covering it up.

Roger had overheard and said, "Don't forget about Troy's birthday. Why don't we just do them together?"

Troy really liked that idea.

Bill asked me, "What do you think, Timmy?"

"Sure!" I really didn't want to share my birthday, especially since I had to do it every year with my mom. But I would have looked like a jerk if I had said no. I had never had my own birthday party until I joined the group a while back when the guys took me to Disneyland and had a big party afterwards. It was the best birthday ever!

Bill told us to decide what we wanted to do. I started telling Troy and Joey what we did last year. I was talking with such enthusiasm that the men started smiling. Troy and Joey were getting really excited.

Then Roger interrupts and said, "We are going to Disneyland this summer, but not for your birthday party."

"Oh," Troy said disappointed, "what can we do?"

"What about a pool party?" Roger offered.

"No," we all answered in unison.

"We all always do that," I said. "What about a big beach party?"

That got everyone's approval.

Bill drove me home later that afternoon. I hadn't had a chance to get some more money from his house, and I only had a little at my house. I thanked Bill for the day, making sure he knew how grateful I was. I guess I was pouring it on too thick because he finally asked, "Timmy, what do you want?"

Oops, I thought. I didn't want him to think I hadn't been genuinely thankful, so I answered, "Nothing, I just wanted to thank you." I got out of the car.

He smiled and pulled away from the curb. Before he went too far, he stopped and backed up. "Timmy, you're so full of shit. How much do you want?"

I laughed and said, "Fifty."

He pulled out his money clip and gave me two twenties.

I yelled thank you and he laughed as he drove away.

Troubled Child

On Sunday night, Mom came into my room and said, "I will be taking you to school tomorrow. I have an appointment with your school principal, Mr. Davies."

"What's it about?" I asked, hoping for a clue. I was shocked she wasn't yelling and screaming and giving me a pre-beating.

True to form, she yelled, "How should I know! But it's about you, so you should be able to figure it out!" Then she slammed the door and left.

That night I could barely sleep. I hated mysteries that included me, especially ones that would probably end in feeling pain.

I went over all I had done wrong at school. I had ditched and gotten into fights. Both were punishable by a beating. Mom had several kinds of beatings. There was the spur of the moment when the rage overcame her and she let loose on you. There was the day's where she was happy and nothing bothered her until she came down off her high and she realized how you had wronged her. Last but not least was the preplanned beating. This one was the worst because she could fashion the weapon of choice before you got home. She had time to listen to the voices in her head and have a hundred reasons why you deserved to be whipped within an inch of your life.

With all this going through my head it was after 3:00 am before I fell asleep. I woke up feeling like a whooped puppy and acting like one. Mom came in the kitchen when I was half done with my bowl of cereal.

"No time for that! Get in the car!" Mom said. On her way to the door, she stopped at the mirror to double-check how good she looked. She always liked to stay in fashion with her clothes and her hairstyle. Today she looked good.

On the way to the school, she started her lecture. "Timmy, I am not putting up with any shit from you! You know how hard your father and I work to put a roof over your head, clothes on your back, and food on the table. You don't appreciate anything! You know I am busy, and now I have to waste a day at your school! "I could tell mom was getting mad and we haven't even got to the school yet. Mom says well, I'll tell you one thing! You better have not disappointed your father and I. Oh shit! I thought I'm dead! Shoot me! As we pulled into the school parking lot we both got out of the car and walked up to the office. The school secretary liked me ever since I beat up the school bully. She told us to have a seat; Mr. Davis would be right with you. Mom graciously smiled and we both took a seat, I sat in the seat right across from her. Mom looked so uncomfortable; she was looking at all the pictures on the wall of all the school founders and all the school principals before Mr. Davis. It was quite intimidating, that's probably why they were up there. All the men looked old, and it made me wonder how Principal Davis' picture would look like on that wall 100 years from now. I laughed to myself, and thought; he's a tall, bold, really fat man." he looked like a character from the "Three Stooges" from TV. No kidding I thought! Then Principal Davis called mom in and we went back to his office. He was very gracious and pulled back a chair for mom to sit in. She thanks him as she sits. Principal Davis points at the seat he wants me to sit in; he didn't have to say anything for me to sit immediately down. Principal Davis sat behind his big desk in a big chair that made him look taller and bigger then he already was. Then he stood up rather quickly. "Mrs. Fielding's, would you like a cup of coffee?" Why yes mom says as she tells Principal Davis how she takes her coffee. Principal Davis fixes mom her coffee, here you are Mrs. Fielding, and gives it to mom. Mom says please, call me Linda. "Very well Linda, then Principal Davis' door opened and a man came in. He was a very tall man, slim, with glasses and gray hair. Principal Davis introduces him to me and my mother as Mr. Burns; he walks over to shake both of our hands. He takes a seat in the chair next to me. Principal Davis says, Mr. Burns is the schools Ldd teacher, it's a program that we believe would greatly benefit Timmy. "What is Ldd?" Mom asks. Principal Davis says it's a program that helps kids that have learning disabilities and social problems. Mom interrupts Principal Davis and says "what are you talking about!" Principal Davis says we have been watching Timmy and testing him for the last three months. He's a problem child Mrs. Fielding's. Moms face turned red, at that I knew I was dead. Principal Davis could see the confused and angry look on moms face; than he says "not in the way you think" Timmy is a kind boy and is always respectful. But he is having trouble keeping up with the other kids. He has a smart mind, but his attention span is very short and he is always distracted and nervous. Linda, I don't know if you know but Timmy goes to the nurse's office at least once a week proclaiming to have a headache. Mind you, the nurse gives him an aspirin and sends him back to class. He's been in at least five fights that we know of. I looked at Principal Davis like why are you trying to get me killed? It's funny I thought, no one keeps track of your fights when you're losing but if you win a few it becomes a big deal! And recently, Principal Davis says; Timmy has been missing a lot of school. When he is here he falls asleep in class, so even when he's here he's not here". At that point I realized I was more than dead, my whole body was shaking. I could see how red moms face was; her whole body was shaking too, just like mine. Hers, because of anger and mine was of fear" Then Principal Davis signed my death certificate. He asked mom something really stupid" Is there a problem at home?" Now you have to understand my mother, she truly believes she's the perfect mom, the perfect wife, she truly believes she can do no wrong. Now mom believes Principal Davis is blaming her for all my problems, she couldn't handle that; she stands up rather quickly as she says "well! I have never been so insulted in all my life! We are a perfectly normal family giving our children a good home and all the love and support they need. Timmy has no problems at home so the problem must be here! With you and your incompetent staff" Principal Davis says, "Linda I didn't mean to insult you, were just trying to get to the bottom of Timmy's problems." Mom looks at me and says, "get up were going." At that mom storms out as I followed her. And I follow her across the parking lot and into the car, in the car she yells at me. "I can't believe you go to a stupid school!" She was so mad she `couldn't see straight. Mom drove really fast all the way home. When mom pulled out of the school parking lot she peeled out really fast, peeling out at every turn, mom yelling at me all the way to the house. The tires screech to a stop. I was so scared; Mom gets out of the car. She stares at me; if looks alone could kill I would be dead. She yells, "Get out of the car!" I do and follow her into the house. She goes into bedroom and slams her door. So I go to mine and sit on the side of my bed just waiting, knowing she would be back to beat me any minute. And the way principle Davis made me sound I knew I had it coming. The worst part is waiting each minute, I anticipated mom bursting into my room with a new rod of pain. I just knew she was in her room wrapping wires together twisting them until she fashioned a whip to tear me apart with. I sat there scared out of my mind for over an hour, actually sweating, ready to break out and cry and beg for mercy. Praying dad would come home or mom would forget anything had happened, but I knew dad was gone for the week and after what principle Davis said about me he would give mom his blessing. I would just be lucky if he didn't whip me after mom did. Finley I couldn't take it any longer, I had been in my room for hours and I was suffocating in fear. I had to find out what mom was up to, where she was at; so I went to my bedroom door and opened it up really slowly and stood there and listened. I didn't hear a sound, the house was really quiet, and I walked through the living room, to the kitchen than the family room but no sign of mom. I walked slowly to mom's room and stood by her door listening for a minute or two. Not a sound, I slowly opened the door at that point. I could hear mom snoring, the room was dark but I could see mom lying in the middle of the bed sleeping. I could also see the bottles of pills on her night stand. She was wasted. I said, mom? She didn't even Move. So I said it just a little bit louder "Mom?" this time she moaned a little bit but she was out of it.

So I walked out quietly, closed the door and knew she would be out of it for a long time if I was lucky she would sleep all day and through the night. But I knew one thing I couldn't see myself sitting in my room waiting for a beating, that would make me go crazy. Plus what difference does it make, it's not like I would get it any worse, mom would give me all she had no matter what the circumstances were.

So I went to the garage and got my bike, started too ride it as fast as I could pass my school to the drugstore. School was still in session and it was still early in the day. I went to the pay phone and with all the people I knew I called Mark. When he answered the phone he was really surprised, probably as surprised as I was to have called him. A couple of weeks ago Mark and I were supposed to go horseback riding together. But I never called him to cancel or explain why I didn't show up.

"Timmy" Mark says, he's kind of caught off guard "I told him, "sorry for not calling sooner, things kind of got crazy"

"Where are you?"

"I'm in front of thrifty drugstore at the pay phone"

"Why aren't you in school?"

"Long story, can you come get me?"

"I guess I can but it's going to take me an hour or so"

Oh I knew I didn't want to stand around, that could be dangerous what if a teacher was to come by. I would be in more trouble than I was already in, I hesitated.

Mark finely says "Look go to the donut shop, I'll be there in 15 min"

"Cool" I said "I will see you there" I hung up the phone figuring I hadn't eaten yet and a donut sounded good. I got on my bike and went further up the street to the donut shop. I got two donuts and a carton of milk. But before I could even sit down Mark was there, I knew who he was and I also knew what kind of guy he is. But I also knew that a guy like him wouldn't let a kid like me get away. He's a small player in my world; there were lots of guys but only a few boys since Mark isn't a major player. He only got to see us boys once a month or pay a lot of money and wait your turn. But today he had a kid knocking on his door, I knew the temptation would be too hard to resist. Plus he seemed like a really nice guy who really listened, plus he had horses that I wanted to ride. Mark got a cup of coffee from the donut shop owner than sat across the table from me.

"Timmy, Mark says I thought I had lost you"

"No you didn't." I smiled at him. I told him about the Palm Springs trip than told him about Phil the body builder and how we made a movie together and bills new studio. I went on and on telling him almost everything.

It was funny, I knew I was talking too much too fast but Mark graciously sat there listening and acted interested in everything I had to say. After I caught him up on everything, I asked him why he didn't play football with us the other day at the park. I told him we had a great time.

Mark just looked at me for the longest time, he took a deep breath and then he surprised me by saying "I thought it would make you feel uncomfortable." I looked at him like he was crazy, I asked, "why would I feel uncomfortable?"

"Well you never called me or came back so I thought something was wrong."

Wow, I thought this guy is way too sensitive. I gave him a real confused look. He finely says "well it doesn't matter." I told him why I wasn't in school and that I didn't fill like sitting around the house waiting for a beating. Mark agrees with me as I finish my donut.

Mark says, "Well Timmy, do you want to go horseback riding?"

"Of course I do!"

I had a real big smile on my face. This time I locked my bike up in front of the donut shop. Then I jump in Mark's car and we took off. I don't know what got into me either, I was excited or nervous or just anxious. I must have talked his ear off. I just kept talking, finely we pulled into Mark's drive way and I was surprised that Mark sat there quietly and listened to every word I had to say just smiling and nodding his head. We both got out of the car and walked to the back where his big barn that housed his horse. It was huge, with a bunch of stalls for all the horses. There were at least a dozen horses. He walked over to a wooden fence where he had around six saddles and Mark showed me what horse I would be riding. I started to pet the horse with my hand, I was stroking her head and I was petting her. I was surprised how soft she was; she really enjoyed the attention I was giving her. Mark was putting a saddle on her; she's a great big beautiful horse. Mark and I started to walk her out; I didn't realize how small I was compared to this big strong horse. I was kind of having second thoughts as we entered the meadow. Mark showed me how to get on the horse, but I couldn't even come close to getting my feet that high to reach the stern up, I was just too small. Finely Mark sees me struggling, he gets behind me picks me up lifts me high and puts me in the saddle. Mark walks me and the horse around telling me the rules, how to go right or left and how to make her walk, stop, or run. Then when he thought I had it down he let her go giving me control at first. The horse just walked, without me having to do a thing. I was really nervous and I believe she picked up on this and started to run. I pulled back on the rains so she would stop but instead she runs faster my feet barley reached the stern up so I bounced around on the saddle. She stops really fast making me fly over her head hitting the ground really hard! (Making me roll on the ground when I came to a stop out of pain and fear I started crying") The horse ran off and Mark ran to me quickly lifting me up off the ground not even asking me where it hurt just telling me to walk it off, he walked me around leading me by my arm toward the horse telling me too stop crying I wiped my face off as mark whistles to the horse and the horse runs too where we were.

"Mark asks, "you ready to try again?" I look at him like he was crazy.

"Look Timmy, if you fall off a horse you have to get right back on I'll ride her with you." so Mark gets on and reaches down for my hand. I give it to him and he lifts me in the saddle in front of him.

"Timmy you'll be fine" will do it together. I'll teach you how to ride like a pro. The horse ride us around on the meadow, Mark telling me everything he thought I should know. Then Mark started making her go faster and faster until she was running really fast. It was fun and with Mark behind me, I felt really safe. I started to relax and have a good time. Mark started walking her again and I could feel him behind me actually smelling my hair, then the back of my neck, it felt weird. But I knew what he wanted even before I called him so I went with it. Mark and I rode the horse back to the barn. We took the saddle off her and then Mark lets her go, the horse walks back to the meadow. Mark decides I need to see the whole barn, including the loft where the hay was. The thing about this guy is he didn't know how to instigate sex with me. I wasn't about to show him. I mean he's been to every party and it's not like we haven't had sex before. He's even on his own turf and it's his barn. But I could see how uncomfortable he is so he has me climb the ladder to the loft as he is right behind me. The loft is full of hay and I expected that this is where mark makes his move.

I'm not scared, just a little nervous. In the loft he holds my face he's telling me the old bull shit! Stuff every other pervert says how good I look, that my body's perfect and that I am a beautiful kid! All the bullshit I was used to hearing but still liked hearing. Hell who wouldn't" Especially a kid that never got a compliment from my parents. Hell they never told me if I was good looking not even if I was cute. But the men in my life always complimented me, they always built me up. And Mark wasn't any different. He poured it on thick, a little too thick. But I notice his hand shaking as he reached around me to pull off my shirt. Then, out of the blue Mark asks, "Do you always get paid?" I smiled and said "yes, always" I wasn't about to say no even though it was a lie I didn't always get paid. Then he looks at me and asked me "is this alright?" I wanted to tell him no for being so stupid! I just want it over with, but I just nod my head yes. Mark takes off his close I could tell he was still nervous. But it didn't stop him, I kick off my shoes. Mark was trying to take my paints off but was having trouble so I help him. He's got a big hard on as he turns me around and bends me over a bale of hay. He was in hard and fast I yelled in pain. He didn't use Vaseline or lotion just his own spit, believe me I paid for riding that horse when he was done with me. We both got dressed and he gives me one hundred dollars and drives me back to my bike without saying a word, until we got to the donut shop. Mark asked "is everything alright?"

"Why! Why wouldn't it be?"

"Can I have your phone number?" He asked.

"Why not I said "He gave me a pen with a piece of paper, so I wright down my name and I put Bills phone number on it. I give it back to him he takes it, thanks me and drives away. I'm thinking, call that number ass hole! I was pissed because when he got what he wanted he was done with me. He didn't want to hang out or anything didn't even really talk to me. I knew it was getting late and I knew it was time to face the music. I started praying mom was still asleep when I got home. I opened the front door real quit like; there was no sound in the house so I close the door just as quietly as I opened it. Still not a sound so I couldn't figure out where she was. So I walked quietly to my room. I notice my bedroom door was open, it was always closed. As I look inside it was clear mom had already taken out her rage on my room. All my clothes were thrown out of my closet along with my shoes and board games; which I never really played with. She had thrown everything across the room taken out all my drawer's out of my chest and dumped them in the middle of the room. She threw all my books off the bookshelves dumped my bed upside down. My room looked like a tornado ripped it apart, but she didn't touch my nightstand that had my stereo on it, that was untouched. Weird I thought, my lamp is across the room, yet nothing Brocken." Than out of the corner of my eye I see mother, she was standing there watching my expression. As I'm looking at what she has done to my room. I turn to face her as she yells "you embarrassed me today! In front of the principal and that teacher" I could see the wire rod in her hand. As she yelling at me! I start crying and begging for mercy, she grabs my hair and throws me to the floor. At this point I'm really scared and really freaked out but I knew this was coming all day. But you can never truly prepare for a beating like this. The first whip caught me in the middle of my back! The pain was more than I could stand. I screamed bloody murder, this throws mom into a frenzy as she swings harder and harder not trying to miss a spot. She works her way down to my ass as I roll up in a ball. She had to kick me a few times to put me into a better position. So she could hit every part of me! Things suddenly went black. The next thing I see is mom standing over me slapping my face, I open my eyes just in time to hear her scream "one hour that's all you get!" If I come back here and this room is a mess it all starts over again! She walks out of my bedroom door and slams it. I'm still crying I couldn't hardly move, the pain seemed unbearable and I could feel the blood running down my face. I had a bloody nose and felt there was blood on my back. This was by far the worst whooping I had ever gotten from my mom. I laid there for the longest time not wanting to move a muscle. Holding my head back to stop my nose bleed, but it didn't make the pain go away and knowing mom would be back to check my room made it worse. Then it hit me, I had a bottle of pain pills that I had gotten from Rick and Todd awhile back. I took the pills out of the bottle and into a plastic bag. I had put them in the insole of a shoe. I made it to my knees; everything was pretty much out of my closet. I looked around on the floor and found it pretty quick; the pills were still there, around ten pills in all. Thank god! I thought one pill knocked me on my ass the last time I took one. So I got one pill and walk very slowly to the bathroom. My head was spinning as I bent over the sink so I could get enough water to swallow the pill. I got a towel for my face and went back to my room. I tried to bend over to pick up some close but it still hurt too much too bend. I needed to let the drug get into my system without falling asleep and I didn't know how to do this. Time wasn't my friend I realized, I had to work through the pain! Crying quietly I sucked it up and started cleaning. I cleaned and cleaned than I realized I wasn't in pain any more. Over an hour had passed and I could barely keep my eyes open and mom never did come back. The room was clean once again. I had to take my shirt off before the blood could dry and stick to my skin. So I got another pill took it into the bathroom and swallowed it before taking my shirt off. Looking in the mirror I could see the damage, it was as bad as I felt I made it to my bed and closed my eyes. Thinking why principle Davis did this to me, I thought he liked me? He loved me when I beat up the school bully! I use to always lose but by the time I was in the fourth grade I had been beat up so many times I was sick of it I thought what the hell, I had nothing to lose. But putting all that aside principle Davis called me slow, I didn't know what he meant by that. At that thought I fell asleep. My sleep was full of pain and bad dreams, of rapes and beatings in the morning. I had forgotten to set my alarm clock for school and no one woke me up, I slept tell around noon. My bed was wet with sweat and I had wet my bed. My sheets were also stained with blood I hurt so bad I could hardly move. So I got to my feet took another pill. I took my sheets off my bed and realized I was naked so I put on a pair of shorts. I knew I had to throw my sheets away. I went to my bedroom door, the house was quiet. I looked out my bedroom window and mom's car wasn't in the drive way. She was gone so I took my sheets to the outside trash can and hid them at the bottom of the trash. Got a pair of clean sheets and put them on my bed. Then sat down on the side of my bed and cried. I'm ten going to be eleven and still wetting the bed. I knew deep down inside it was the beating and pain pill that made me sleep through it. The pill started to kick in and it was easy to fall back to sleep.

I slept till late that night. I was in pain and really hungry and thirsty. I took another pill and went to the kitchen. It was two in the morning so I knew I wouldn't run into mom. There was fried chicken on a plate. I got a few pieces, some mashed potatoes and a glass of milk. I didn't want to make any noise so I ate it cold. As I was eating I realized I haven't even faced dad yet! I knew mom had probably already called him and why wouldn't she? I was in the wrong I had embarrassed mom and dad! And for the first time in my life I felt like my dad started to like me, he saw that I had friends. Bill had met dad, even giving dad side jobs so he could make extra money. And Bill introduced dad to a pro baseball player who gave dad a lot of side jobs. All this was done because I knew Bill and Dad knew this, it made our relationship a little better. It's funny a few months ago mom played a song for dad (The cat's in the cradle and the silver spoon, the little boy blue and the man on the moon) That song really made dad fill guilty for never being home. So every time dad remembered the song or mostly mom reminded him, he would tell us kids he loved us. Mom would tell us she loved us too, but her love was very scary, violent and full of rage! I felt like I lived on the edge . . . And can't see a way out of my life. I was stuck and knew there was nothing I could do, nothing new there. I needed to do what worked in the past. Just put it out of my mind and try to act like this was normal, my head started spinning the pill was taking affect and I felt so alone.

I hope you enjoyed <u>Untold Secrets</u>. It was really hard writing this book, my child hood memories are still very painful. But it's a story I thought had to be told. My next book is really scary but it has a great ending. '<u>Escaping child abuse</u>'